# WHAT AM I?

# WHAT AM I?
# A STUDY IN NON-VOLITIONAL LIVING

## Galen Sharp

Tandava Press

ISBN: 0987380613

ISBN-13: 978-0-9873806-1-6

Cover Design by Lewis Agrell
Author's photo by Glenn Cuerden
Edited by Tony Cartledge

**What Am I?** A Study in Non-Volitional Living / by
Galen Sharp

Tandava Press
www.tandavapress.com
info@tandavapress.com

Printed in the United States of America

To Terence James Stannus Gray, aka Wei Wu Wei.
Though this is not as concise nor as eloquent
nor as profound as what you have given to us,
it is this sentient being's attempt to thank you and
honor you.

"To-o-wha-a-t, to-o-wh-a-t, to-o-who-o-o-om,
replied the owl to the rabbit."

*Terence Gray as O.O.O.*
*"Unworldly Wise, as the owl remarked to the rabbit"*

# ACKNOWLEDGMENTS

To Tony Cartledge, my editor, for his sensitivity to content and ability to help clarify complex passages and enthusiastic dedication to the book.

To David Rivers, my publisher, and Natasha Rivers for their hard work, understanding, and commitment to bring this book to print.

To Bobbie Sharp, my wife, for her insightful suggestions and excellent advice, proof reading help and unfailing encouragement.

To Larry Smitherman, my friend, for his beautiful book layout and typographic design.

Without them I would have only a large computer file and the reader would not have this book.

# CONTENTS

# INTRODUCTION

"Thirty years ago we thought that we were heading towards an ultimate reality of a mechanical kind. Today there is a wide measure of agreement, which on the physical side of science, approaches almost to unanimity, that the stream of knowledge is heading towards a non-mechanical reality; the universe begins to look more like a great thought than a great machine. *Matter is derived from consciousness, not consciousness from matter.*" (emphasis added)

–Sir James Jeans

(*Physics and Beyond* by Werner Heisenberg).

Are you ready for an intriguing adventure into some new and virtually unexplored territory? As you can see from the title, this is a different kind of book about some very different ideas. It explores a variety of subjects such as science, philosophy, quantum physics and even some of the ancient masters in quest of a higher way of knowing the world and ourselves. And through the eleven Reality Meditations you will be able to examine your own mental mechanisms and find out how they really work, examine who and what you really are, and discover why you are here.

If you are a bit of a non-conformist this book may appeal to that. And if you like paradoxes and mysteries it will fascinate you also. In any case you will need a sense of wonder as well as a sense of adventure. For the point is not just to be different or mysterious, but to actually open our perception to a higher dimension. This is not just a figure of speech or merely a new metaphor for something conventional, but an actual realm existing at this moment along with the world we now observe. This New Reality is, of course, not new in itself. It has been spoken of and sought for thousands of years. It is, however new to most people.

Once you become aware of this higher reality you will also recognize others who have arrived before you. This is not some kind of elitist or superior group, though many have sought it unsuccessfully for that reason. Those who live in this reality may not even appear as anyone different to the general population, but you will know them. And, by the same token, you may attract some new friends.

My own transformation began when I started asking the same questions we explore in this book. I discovered that what I called reality was formed from a world model I was taught when I was young, and it wasn't real at all. I also discovered that it was the reason behind my lack of fulfillment and all of my unhappiness and frustration. As you find this out for yourself and contemplate the Reality Meditations you will also begin to see the world differently and your mind will begin to operate in a new way —

whole, unconditioned and spontaneous, the way it was meant to operate.

However, you must see this for yourself. You must look for yourself and discover it for yourself. No one can do this for you.

But that is what makes it an adventure.

# HUMANITY'S
# NEXT STEP?

In the classic film *2001: A Space Odyssey*, written by Stanley Kubrick and Arthur Clark, man discovered the Stargate[1] and attained a new, higher level of consciousness which opened a higher dimension to their perception. The film presented higher consciousness as a plausible next step for humankind.

The beginning depicts Homo Sapiens' previous step up from the ape, from primitive awareness to a new kind of consciousness incorporating rational thought and a developed concept of self. It suggests that something happened to the ape mind to initiate a new mode of functioning, which initiated the era of the thinking primate. As the film continues, humans – after fully developing this new function – are able to reach outer space and the Stargate,

---

1. A somewhat different version of this chapter by the author appeared in *New Realities* magazine in January of 1980 under the title, S*targate: Humanity's next glorious step?*

which opened yet another more profound quality of awareness.

Many of us are captured by a similar hope, the vision that something of the sort actually does lie ahead for us. It has also been suggested that in order to understand mystical and psychical experiences we must search for a new model of reality, a higher world-view that incorporates a paradigm which allows room for the spiritual and the mystical.

## *Scientific Progress Toward A New Model Of Reality*

The leading edge of scientific investigation is now in the field of high-energy particle physics, which, it is hoped, will lead to an understanding of the basic structure of matter. The belief is that this will be the key to the mysteries of the universe. Some physicists also hope it will answer many of the questions regarding mystical and paranormal experiences and open the way to a higher consciousness.

One important aspect of modern physics is the search for a unified field theory. This would bring together the four (known) basic forces of nature – electromagnetism, gravity, weak and strong nuclear forces – and unite them in one balanced equation. It would mean that the four fundamental forces are all one, yet manifested in different ways. However, a unified field theory has yet to be completed to the satisfaction of most physicists. In fact, the deeper they delve into the atom the stranger things become. Things happen that no longer fit into our conventional, physical, mechanistic view of reality.

For instance, Sir Arthur Eddington's illustration of the shadow table reveals that there is "nothing physical in the entire universe, just fields of forces." Eddington, in his book, *The Nature of the Physical World* describes his table in scientific terms as "mostly emptiness, sparsely scattered in the emptiness are numerous electric charges rushing about with great speed ... there is a vast difference between my scientific table with its substance (if any) thinly scattered in specks in a region mostly empty and the table of everyday conception which we regard as the type of solid reality. (p. xii-xiii.) He also says: "The revelation by modern physics of the void within the atom is more disturbing than the revelation by astronomy of the immense void of interstellar space."

A proven aspect of the Heisenberg uncertainty principal declares that the observer is not separate from the particle observed. As Sir James Jeans sums up in the quote on page XV, physicists are almost unanimous that we are heading towards revelations of a non-mechanical reality. Now compare these modern, scientific observations with this quote from the ninth century Ch'an master, Hsi Yün (Huang Po): "From the first to the last not even the smallest grain of anything perceptible (or tangible) has ever existed or ever will exist." And also, "Moreover, in thus contemplating the totality of phenomena, you are contemplating the totality of

Mind." (*The Zen Teachings of Huang Po.* John Blofeld, translator).

Not only are our everyday notions of materiality being shattered but there also seems to be increasing evidence of a basic oneness underlying all phenomenality and the consciousness of the observer.

## Oneness And Consciousness

The theory of the essential oneness of all nature and consciousness is, of course, not unique to modern physics. It is a belief that runs through Eastern as well as Western mysticism. And the idea actually grows in strength and emphasis as it is followed back to more ancient belief systems.

Science now reluctantly admits that consciousness itself is a key factor of physical manifestation at the most basic level. They have at least recognized that consciousness is involved in and actually able to cause the manifestation of phenomenality (as we will explore in the chapter *A New Paradigm*). A better understanding of this connection will help open the way to move into a new, higher relationship with the physical universe.

Physicist Niels Bohr comments: "Consciousness must be a part of nature, or, more generally, of reality, which means that, quite apart from the laws of physics and chemistry, as laid down in quantum theory, we must also consider laws of quite a different kind ... Here we obviously have a genuine case of complementarity, one that we shall have to analyze in greater detail ..." (*Physics and Beyond*).

The growing attention to the factor of consciousness and the basic oneness of all phenomenality in modern physics is leading us right to the doors of metaphysics, much to the discomfort of some theorists. We are being forced to revise our conventional, physical, space-time view of reality even more radically than we were with the Einsteinian revolution.

## *Approaching A New Model Of Reality*

The popular term "higher consciousness" actually reveals a basic misunderstanding of the nature of consciousness. Consciousness itself does not change for it is not a "thing." Rather, it is actually the manner of cognitive functioning, or cognition, that is different. Humankind's first elevation of cognition required a fundamental transformation in the way the mind actually functioned. This new ability for conceptual, rational thought triggered a new world-view, a new way to relate to the world. After that, all progress in understanding has been on this conceptual level and is a product of the rational thought mechanism. But there remains yet another higher mode in which the mind can function. And we are now on the verge of another momentous change in the way the mind itself operates.

In our present approach to science and philosophy we have been trying to take the faculty of rational, conceptual thought to greater lengths in the assumption that this higher level of understanding will come by developing even more complicated concepts. However, since our first great leap up from the ape required a change in the basic way the mind itself functioned, is it not probable the next great leap will also require something no less radical? This next step could be as incomprehensible to our present mind as conceptual, rational thought is to the animals.

## *The New Reality Is Here, Now*

Fortunately, to find the New Reality we do not have to look, as in the movie *2001: A Space Odyssey*, to outer space, we can find it right here and now. This reality has been with us all along. Indeed, many have already entered. A new kind of human is already appearing, unnoticed by the general population.

According to ancient Ch'an teachings there actually is another higher manner in which the mind can function where the entire universe, including oneself, is recognized in its basic wholeness. One actually *is* the universe, and the barriers of space and time fall away.

These ancient writings fit in surprisingly well with the recent turns of scientific investigation. However, unlike modern science, these ancient texts say this higher functioning is reached not by pressing the conceptual, rational processes even further, but, curiously enough, by simply rediscovering the original more "primitive," non-conceptual, non-dual mode of awareness. This is the kind of awareness we had before the conceptual thought mechanism began to function.

These writings also tell us that in abandoning this earlier awareness to develop conceptual thought and the self-concept, we have forgotten important, unique qualities it contained. Babies and very young children still possess this more fundamental form of awareness and go through an evolution of cognition as they grow up, by learning conceptual thought and acquiring a self-concept. The previous mode of awareness is then totally forgotten. A young child cannot and does not observe or recognize this early mode of cognition at the time. This is simply because the child has nothing to compare it with. They just live it. However, if it is again returned to *from* the fully-developed conceptual mode it is instantly recognized and remembered.

Ironically, the New Reality may actually be reached by recovering our original mode of cognition after first fully developing the second mode. A third, far higher mode, then appears as a synergism of the first two.

An integration of the two ways of cognition has the effect of bringing about something infinitely higher than each mode of cognition individually. Therefore, the recovery of the original mode of cognition is not really a step backward but a profound leap forward through the incorporation of both. Our present rational, linear, conceptual thought mode may have been a necessary step, but it is not the ultimate step. It has almost reached its practical limits. And it has now in fact become a barrier to further progress.

The present scientific methodology now moves only along the second level of cognition, ignoring the first level because it has been entirely forgotten and is veiled by the conceptual thought mechanism. This is because our conceptual thought processes work dualistically through the comparison of opposites. The previous non-dual level does not operate in this manner; being intuitional and non-linear it assimilates all perceptions without differentiation and views the universe as aspects of one's observable self. One's self is not viewed as a thing or separate entity nor even as a part of some greater whole. Because of this dividing or splitting process the linear, conceptual mind, while thinking, is a "split-mind." Through split-mind (our present mode of mind) we see the world fragmented into things: this-that, self-other, here-there, before-after, and so on. We, in thought, seem to be a thing apart from a world of other things, trapped in time and space. We are a house divided against itself.

Because of the peculiar way the rational thought mechanism operates, the world most of us live in is not the actual world as we once knew it in our original awareness as a small child. Deep down we know this. It has instead become a world of mental labels. Our thought processes automatically take our stream of percepts, categorize them and label them. We habitually relate to the labels instead of the living perception. Categorizing and labeling is the function of conceptual thought and it has taken us far. However, our focus of consciousness and thus our interpretation of the world is not as it truly is, as we once lived it as a child. Now we know it only by the labels, the symbols of thoughts and concepts created by the thought mechanism. We have even made ourselves into one of these labels.

Now, it may seem difficult to realize and to accept the fact that we know ourselves entirely as mere thoughts and are not seeing our actual essence, but a simple experiment may help drive it home. We may ask ourselves: "What am I?" Notice that thoughts of what we are immediately arise. Yet we could never be any of those thoughts. Why? *Because a thought can't think.*

Instead, we could inquire: "Where do thoughts come from?" Finding this source should reveal what we are. But when we try to look, we automatically look for the source of thought in even more complicated thoughts and ideas. This experiment may be a bit confounding, though after a few moments reflection it should at least become apparent that we must be something much more wondrous than any self we can ever think of or conceptualize, no matter how intricate and profound our ideas.

The effects of this labeling process by our thought mechanism have put us in a precarious position with disastrous consequences. It has created a host of unconscious mental barriers and limitations, trapping us firmly in time and space.

We have become alienated from our own original, infinite self, and consequently from our fellow sentient beings and from nature. The rational human thought mechanism that elevates us above the animals may seem to be our ultimate achievement but it has exacted a price.

"The Enlightened being is totally identified with the entire universe," is a typical Ch'an principle. Through our present mental processes, we have left reality. We have become split into an intellectual "self," which controls a "me" and also controls nature. Through our rationalism we have transformed ourselves into mere labels, abstract mental "things," isolated from our fellow "things" and from nature. To "have" and to "control" have replaced simply being what we actually are but have forgotten. Having become pale ghosts of our true nature living in a nether world of concepts and labels, we have completely lost the ability to experience total, pure, limitless being and have become increasingly frustrated, depressed, and desperate.

These ancient writings reveal that a "whole-mind" is realized when the mind ceases to be split and becomes whole – reintegrated, unlimited, infinite – and begins to function from its original, unconditioned spontaneity. These texts say that this is a unique way of living that is neither a form of license nor living by tenets, codes of behavior or will power. It is called *non-volitional living* and is essentially effortless and absolutely free.

This is the ultimate liberation. It is at once wholeness with all creation and a non-attachment to the frustrations, insecurities and limitations of the conceptual, false self. We may then discover we are neither the mortal, thought-formed self nor *anything else*. Rather, as the writings say, we are the "light of pure consciousness" in and by which everything appears, from the nearest thought to the furthest galaxy. Even time and space dissolve as mere concepts.

## Entering Into The New Reality

Entering the New Reality is deceptively simple in description. However, our present mode of mind function constantly thwarts and misdirects us, as you may find if you attempt it yourself. This is the process: the two modes of consciousness – split-mind and whole-mind – may appear antithetical to the conceptual mind, but by comprehending both at the same time a synergistic effect is triggered and a revolutionary new understanding of one's self and the physical world is revealed.

How does this happen? We cannot make it happen, but we can open ourselves to allow it to happen. It can happen in an instant as we return our full focus of consciousness "upstream" of the conceptual thought process and the labels we construct, and recognize or re-cognize what we actually are. It will be unlike anything we may be expecting or anything we can imagine. We will discover that we are quite different from what our thought mechanism tells us we are. We will recognize our timeless original being and our actual wholeness and oneness with all creation.

We can begin by closely and attentively examining how our own thought mechanism works. Then we can eventually begin to understand how and why it automatically fragments the world and divides us from it spatially and temporally. Through this kind of investigation we can expose our bondage to the illusory, capricious pseudo-self invented by the dualistic thought process. When this is deeply understood it will then allow us to refocus our conscious attention "upstream" of the thought process and apperceive our original, free, non-dual Source.

When this happens we will simply recognize what we always have been. We will discover we are not what we *thought* we were. Yet, we will become nothing that we weren't already. Pursued diligently, this seemingly innocuous line of observation can bring one to literally mind-altering and life-transforming discoveries. This kind of simple attention to the thought mechanism and how it affects the way we see the world and ourselves can, of itself, lead to profound new insights.

For those interested in symbols, try this. Draw a forward slanting line upward to represent the original non-linear mode of cognition. / Then draw another line down from that line to represent the present linear, conceptual mode. \ And then draw a line from the bottom of this line back to the bottom of the first line to represent the return and Awakening. This creates a triangle, a triad, a trinity, a pyramid. ∆ This was an ancient symbol of Pure Consciousness and also represented the door to Awakening. Recovering this original form of cognition opens the way to a radically different perspective of the physical universe and of "mind power," unattainable to the conceptual mind. From this new, higher perspective can come marvelous, new discoveries. But much more important is the new, effortless way of living and the vast sociological implications of a world where we are not all struggling amongst ourselves but see others as aspects of what-we-are.

# WHAT ARE YOU?

## *Doing The Reality Meditations*

Real, awakened life is effortless and spontaneous. You might think of the accompanying Reality Meditations as "reality experiments" that will allow you to see what-you-are and that everything that appears is actually an aspect of what-you-are.

It is not necessary to feel that you thoroughly understand each chapter before you go on to the next one. The study encapsulated in this book can be approached from many directions and something further on may be the key for you. Keep going then come back and go through it again.

You are greatly encouraged to actually *do* each Reality Meditation at the beginning of the next eleven chapters. They are ones that I have found to be the most effective and powerful through years of testing in seminars and workshops. Repeat them after reading the chapter. Just reading them or imagining them is not enough because they are designed to work on a different level than your linear intellectual process. They can accomplish what mere words cannot. By actually doing them, you are communicating with your deeper non-linear understanding. This is essential for true insight. And you may well get your first actual experience of the New Reality while doing one of these experiments. Many have.

As the noted sage Douglas Harding says of such experiments: "Just reading them and not doing them is like eating the menu instead of the meal."

## Reality Meditation # 1
## The I Chart

**Make a chart of** who you are.  Start with your name at the top and labels down the left side.

Name?
Where do I live?
Where was I born?
What is my gender?
What do I look like physically?
What are my hobbies?
Am I married?
Do I have children?

What are my treasures?
What are my strengths?
What are my weaknesses?
What are my most important accomplishments?

What is my best memory?

What is my worst memory?

This is who you think you are.

Now, ask yourself these questions: (Don't rush them. Pause for a while with each one and really focus on it. Try to look deeper than your first assumption.)

1. Is this really me?

2. Or is this simply a list of labels, ideas, memories, concepts?

3. If I had no labels would I still exist?

4. Who or what would I be then?

5. Does this thought upset me?

6. Instead of focusing on your label self, why not speculate upon what your "True Self" could be?

## *What Are You?*

> *A dunce once searched for a fire*
> *with a lighted lantern.*
> *Had he known what fire was*
> *He could have cooked his meal much sooner."*
>
> — Mumon

Most of us assume we are living in the "real" world and believe no one could convince us otherwise. For what other world is there? The reality of this solid three-dimensional world we see as "other than me" that was here before we were born and will exist after we die, is indisputable for 99.99% of the population. So is the assumption of this individual "me" who is living in it. It all seems to be self-evident.

This book is about how I made the rare discovery that *that* world is not the "real world." And that "me" is not the "real me." It is a world of illusion, frustration and suffering. This book is about how that illusory world can be exposed and dissolved.

Our aim here is not about getting the right philosophy or the right religion or the right doctrine. I'm talking about something astonishing that can be discovered in the everyday here-and-now when we simply try to investigate what-we-are. This is not something new that I have invented. It is an ancient secret I came upon which actually

activated a new, higher mental process that transformed my life.

## *I Did It My Way ... And It Didn't Work*

When I was 18 years old I had a relationship
with a girlfriend that ended badly. She dumped me.
Looking back I can hardly blame her. She was a
wonderful girl, but I was troubled about life. I was
brooding and self-centered, depressed, frustrated,
and filled with self-doubt. Life wasn't going the
way I thought it should go, and that episode just
confirmed it all the more.

So I began reading books about philosophy
and the human condition. But that only made
things worse. I just found more idiotic ideas about
how things should be, and became even more frustrated. While brooding that the world is unjust is
not so unusual for a teenager, my case was perhaps
more severe.

But I did have a deep sense of wonder along
with a sense of adventure. I was in my last year of
high school when I got the brilliant idea that I could
find some answers and thus possible happiness by
going to Europe. I didn't have any money, so I took
a job in an art store to earn enough to buy a boat
ticket, without thinking about how I'd live when I
got there.

In those days ocean liners were still crossing
to Europe and though it took two weeks to make the
crossing from New York to Le Havre, France, it was
quite a bit cheaper than air travel which had just

recently become available. And I had a lot more time than money. I had already looked into trying to work my way across on a steamer, but found that just wasn't available to young vagabonds any more. Even if you could get a job on a boat you had to sign up for the round-trip, and I was just going one way.

I arrived in Paris with forty dollars in my jeans and my own romantic naiveté to propel me on. And I did have quite a time. It was good for me to be on my own. I gained a lot of self-assurance and a more mature perspective, but I did starve a lot. (I weighed only 54kg / 120lb. when I returned home two years later.) I had worked one summer as an illustrator for an advertising agency before I left home, so when I could, I earned money sketching peoples' portraits in restaurants and bars. And, since I also had some experience doing animated cartoons, I was able to work two summers in Stockholm for an animation studio.

At the end of the first summer I was afraid it would be too cold to spend the winter in Sweden, so I started hitch-hiking south again to find a warmer climate. Besides, it had gotten hard for me to spend very long in any one place. I met a number of people who had started out like me, but found that they could not quit wandering. They had become old men roaming from place to place experiencing what they could and then moving on in anticipation of new and different adventures.

I had made it down as far as Barcelona, Spain when I met a young traveler who had planned to meet a friend on the Canary Islands, off the coast of

North Africa and sail on his boat through the Panama Canal and on to Tahiti.

However the traveler wasn't going to be able to make it, and asked me if I was interested in taking his place. That fit perfectly with my fantasy of living in a hut on a tropical island with a beautiful native girl and I jumped at the opportunity.

He gave me his friend's name and wrote him a note introducing me and explaining the situation. I hitch-hiked on to Cadiz at the entrance to the Mediterranean where I spent my last 10 dollars on a boat ticket to Las Palmas de Gran Canaria.

Since I was broke and hungry when I arrived, I sat down in the middle of the city square, put my clarinet together and began playing a kind of extemporaneous be-bop jazz that I liked to perform. Soon a large group of people were gathered around clapping their hands and having a good time. Somebody started passing around a plate and in a half hour I had collected enough pesetas for a loaf of bread, some wine and a cot in the local flop house. A few days later I was secretly allowed to sleep on the couch of the island's art school, *The Escuela Lujan Perez,* by some of the more avant-garde art students who considered themselves representatives of the island's counter-culture. They were very kind and generous to me even though they had very little themselves.

It was there, late one night while I was in a state of drunken self-pity that I wrote in my diary something that turned out to be quite prophetic. I wrote: "I can never be happy until my ideals become reality ... or reality becomes my ideal." I hesitated after the first part – realizing that there was another possibility, that reality could also be one's ideal. At the time, of course, I assumed that the only satisfactory answer to my problems would be that my ideals would become a reality.

It took me many years to realize that that very assumption *was* my problem. What I wanted was impossible. And the only feasible possibility was that reality must become my ideal. But, naturally, at eighteen when I wrote that, it was beyond my consideration. I didn't like the reality I was experiencing. I only knew that I wanted the world to go *my way* – at least once in a while. Little did I realize that I didn't even know what reality was.

I never did get to Tahiti. But that's another story.

### The One False Assumption

The key question which neither philosophy nor religion hardly ever asks is: "What am I?" All the popular religious, philosophical, even the New Age beliefs simply assume without question that we are an individual, personal, volitional entity – an autonomous self. It is felt that to believe otherwise would be tantamount to suicide, virtually unthinkable. It's downright un-American. We can't even imagine what it could be like to not be an individual entity. Frankly, it scares us and is to be avoided at all costs.

To even question the idea of a self is impossible for most people to do. For wouldn't that be giving up control and personal responsibility? But we shall discover that the best control is to not desire control. In reality, we will find that it is actually the concepts of self and volition that put us out of control. But what makes us so sure we even have a self in the first place? Have we ever really looked for it?

There is a higher way of living in which we spontaneously and effortlessly live as we have aspired to do. However, there is a catch: we have to lose our life to find it. That is, we have to lose our false life to find our real life. In this context the term "lose" does not mean "to get rid of." It simply means to see through it as you would see through an illusion or a magician's trick when you find out how it is done. When that happens, the illusion disappears of itself.

It is very rare that we ever really question who and what we are. And when we do, we usually get bogged down in a tangle of philosophical questions and end up more confused than ever. Indeed, it can be such a spooky thing that we learn to avoid even thinking about it. In fact, most of us are convinced that we already know who and what we are. This is deceptive because when we are asked we really can't locate it, let alone articulate it. It's one of those things that we have learned to avoid by convincing ourselves that we already know.

For most of us the term "our true self" means how we truly think and feel deep down when we peel away our layers of false images and social conditioning. That is the kind of thing we learn in those touchy-feely groups where we "get in touch with our feelings and explore our real emotions." But that's only about thinking and feeling. It still doesn't really answer the basic, concrete question: "What am I?" What actually is it that is doing the thinking and feeling?

## A Simple Experiment

If and when we actually do look for what we are, all we can find are concepts and ideas. Try this yourself right now. Put this book down and look for an actual self that isn't just a thought or a feeling.

What did you find?

You see, you must go deeper than concepts, ideas and feelings to try to find the actual source of it all.

I had toyed with this question before, though I had never seriously dealt with it. But eventually I reached a point in my life where, after working very hard, I had achieved some of the major goals in my life (I was also working eighty-plus hours a week). I had married a lovely woman, I had two beautiful children and I was a successful illustrator and creative director for a national advertising agency. Yet, I was still not feeling fulfilled. I was still not happy.

In questioning why, I tried to imagine what it would actually take for me to live a happy, fulfilling life. Every scenario I would imagine fell short and I had to keep taking it a step further. By doing this I realized, to my utter dismay, that even if I were the ruler of the entire world I still wouldn't be happy.

This was because I still would not be able to make everything go the right way, my way. Things would still go wrong. Nor could I even live up to my own ideals and values. I would still have to struggle. And then I thought, who was I that I even deserved to be happy? Most of the people in the world today are struggling day-to-day just to stay alive. Compared to them I was just a spoiled crybaby. I was fortunate to have things as good as I did. But, knowing that didn't make me happy. Guilty, perhaps, because I wanted more, but not happy. I had to face the fact that quite possibly I would never be happy and fulfilled.

The result was a deep, lasting depression.

I began to question everything. And that's what ultimately led me to the question of what I was. I realized that, like most people, I had unconsciously assumed that my labels were what defined me – labels such as "human being," "father," "artist," "husband," etc. In other words, I identified with my self-concept. This also included my accomplishments and failures and my values. But the important thing was that I had begun to explore the question: "What am I?"

## The Turning Point In My Life

I began to ponder this question every spare moment I had, I became consumed by it. After months of continual, steady focus upon this one question, I was very fortunate one day to realize, during a timeless moment of clarity, that who I had accepted as "me," as what I was, was just a concept. Nothing more. Therefore a concept couldn't be a person – it was just a thought. And *a thought can't think*. So that conceptual person couldn't be who was thinking. Also, concepts can change moment to moment, and my concept of myself depended upon how I felt at the moment – what I was thinking about at the moment, how other people were treating me and how well I was doing at that instant. It shifted and changed like the sands in the desert; it had no true substance, no stability. I saw that I could not be that.

No wonder I could never feel happy or fulfilled, let alone secure. I was identifying myself with an ever-changing, unstable illusion: my self-concept.

To realize that what I had always assumed I was is not really me, but just a concept, just a thought, was actually incredibly liberating. I realized that I had been spending most of my life as a slave to an ever-shifting, ever-vulnerable concept of myself, trying to please and satisfy this concept and keep it looking good. I had mistaken the imaginary for the actual, and all those needs and fears had their source in that illusion. I realized that this imaginary self's problems were not actually my problems. This lifted a huge burden from me, and the relief was incredible.

## The First Step

If you can see this truth for yourself, not just intellectually, but deeply and completely, you have already taken the first step. You apprehend that a concept is not the living actuality, but just the dead symbol, an illusion. The concept is not the actual thing but just an imaginary idea of it, a hazy, capricious mental image of it.

For instance, we can have the concept, or even the memory, of a tree, but the actual perceptual experience of the tree is the reality. The concept "tree" is not the actual, it is just a mental image, a dead symbol.

Our concept of "tree" may change, or how we think of a tree may change moment to moment, but that doesn't actually affect any real trees. It only affects the way we think of them or feel about them.

What this means is that we don't live and react from our real self, but from our imagination of it. We don't live in the actual world, but *in our thoughts about it*. We live in an unstable, shifting illusion. And, believe it or not, that is the source of all our problems. Yes, *all* of them.

I had been making the same mistake that 99.99% of the people in the world make: I had mistaken the dead concept for the living actuality.

But this was also very puzzling to me at the same time because, while I had discovered what I wasn't, I could not figure out what I really was. The answer to that secret was so incredibly simple, so obvious and yet so wondrous that it took me years to discover. Most people never find it. That's because they believe they already know the answer. And they don't want different answers, that would be too confusing. But that's why they are unfulfilled. And why they never even think to ask the question: "What am I?" It is why they never know their *real life*, their real being, real fulfillment and totally effortless reality. The real world is where everything is always as it should be.

I could have easily spent my life futilely chasing after fulfillment and happiness through my accomplishments, my possessions and my self-image, virtually a slave to the concept of "me" while real fulfillment was always freely and effortlessly available right here and right now.

One of the reasons this higher reality works is because we don't have to force ourselves to believe in some utopian dream. We don't have to remember a bunch of principles that we have to remember to apply. In fact, we don't have to remember to *do* anything. Instead, we simply have to honestly look and investigate the "cold, hard facts" around us. This will inexorably lead us into a concrete reality so solid and so powerful that it will literally replace the old unworkable model all by itself.

You don't have to "kill the ego" or "die to self" as you may have been told. Ego is *already* dead. But you haven't realized this because you assume you *are* this imaginary "me." You don't know who or what you really are and so you are identifying with a concept of yourself. You are actually asleep – a sleep-walking zombie stumbling around in an insubstantial dream-world of concepts and labels. But you can discover your true being. You can wake up and enter a new realm in a higher dimension.

## *Awakening*

The highest and best of the ancient masters called this "awakening" because that's exactly what it is. But that term has since been misunderstood by those still asleep and carelessly used to mean many fanciful things. It is not a matter of faith, spirituality or self-perfection as you may have thought, or even of a special esoteric knowledge. It is, in fact, a matter of simply questioning some of your most basic assumptions. It is not a matter of adopting someone else's belief system, but of simply looking honestly and fearlessly at the here-and-now and reaching your own conclusions. And by doing so, losing your pain-causing illusions.

Moving into reality has nothing to do with strict disciplines, or religion, or New Age pseudoscience. It is not learning something new and mystical, but looking openly at what is here-and-now and discovering it for yourself. It is something you can do as you go about your normal daily round. You don't have to change anything about yourself or your life.

As discovery happens, the changes happen by themselves. When you really see for yourself what is here-and-now rather than what you have been taught to assume, then illusions fall away by themselves and the real world is gradually revealed as it has always been but was hidden by your own mirage.  You will actually ascend from a lower dimension of confusion, pain, and fear to the higher dimension of peace, fulfillment, and reality.

## *The Current Consensus Model Of Reality Is Based On False Assumptions*

No matter how good our philosophies are, we forget to apply them from moment to moment in daily life and so don't really live by them.  In fact, no matter how noble, lofty, and inspired our beliefs and values, we still find ourselves acting contrary to them and wonder why. How often have we been told to love one another?  We may well agree, but when it really gets down to it we really can't do it.  We don't know how; we haven't the ability; we simply forget.  It's not just a matter of conjuring up some warm, fuzzy, loving feelings now is it?  Actually, loving one another is what we think *others* need to do.  And instead of liberating us as we thought they would, our noble beliefs actually become a job and a burden of guilt.  In fact, the higher our values, the more we fall short of them.  And we are encouraged to "just try harder."  But the answer is neither to try harder nor to lower our values.  The problem is that our current model of reality actually causes us to work against our self.

We think that all we need is to be told the right way to think and act and believe and then we can do it.  That's an illusion.  Never trust anyone else to tell you what to think, no matter how successful and self-assured they may appear.

Now, do Reality Meditation #1 once again.

# MINDSET

## *Reality Meditation # 2*
## The Now Experiment

**W**ithout personalizing or judging anything try the following exercise.

If thoughts carry you off, as soon as you notice them, don't fight them, simply ignore them and return to the now.

First, *listen*. What sounds are you hearing? It may be traffic outside, voices in the next room, a radio in the distance, sounds of nature. The point is to notice every nuance of sound.

Second, *feel*. Start with your feet and move up your body. Notice what your shoes feel like, the feel of the chair under you, your arms and hands, your neck, head, face, the feel of your clothing on your body.

Third, *see*. Notice the room about you, any movement, objects.

Take it all in. What's happening?

Fourth, *smell*. Is there a scent in the air?

Fifth, *taste*. Is there a taste in your mouth?

Say the word "now" to yourself. Be in it. Stay here awhile and just *be*.

We have probably noticed all these things before in bits and pieces, but we rarely put them all together. If we really notice any of these things it is in brief snatches between other thoughts of this and that.

Did you perhaps relax just a bit as you were doing the experiment? Maybe you noticed your neck and shoulder muscles loosened. You might have found that anxieties lessened and disturbing thoughts ceased to intrude for a brief spell. If you happen to be outdoors it will probably enhance the effect. Being in nature seems to expand our awareness.

Try to do this experiment as often as you can remember during the day. You will begin to notice something magical, a familiar specialness. It is a point of contact with *life* in the purest sense of the word. It may take a while to generate this contact, especially if you are in a tense emotional state, but keep it up. There is more *here* than we have first assumed.

After doing the now experiment, consider these questions:

1. Where do you spend most of your *mental life*?

     a. Thoughts of past events, rethinking them – 1 to 100% of the time

     b. Imaginations of future events, anticipating – 1 to 100%

    c. The present moment, living now – 1 to 100%

2. Which is most real: a, b, or c?

3. Could you be missing your real life?

4. Why? (Are you trying to rationalize the past, anticipate the future?)

5. Where does most of your mental strain come from: past, future or present?

6. Which do you prefer: a, b, or c? Why?

7. How can you live more consistently in the present?

## Mindset

*"We are never deceived;*
*we deceive ourselves."*
—Goethe

## Why It Is Difficult To Maintain An Open Mind

Perceiving the here-and-now will be very difficult at first. That is because of our *mindset*. Mindset works like an automatic perception filter for our learned world-view, also called our world model or our model of reality. New ideas that question our self or our volition go against our mindset. It feels threatening. We like our self in spite of it's flaws. We think it is all we have and feel like we would literally be lost without it. And the very last thing we want to do is to try to pretend to ignore it or try to be "selfless." But, we will find that instead of being lost without it, we have been lost *because of it*.

Our mindset has virtually blinded us to the obvious within the here-and-now. That's how it keeps us prisoner. Terence Gray, a fully-awakened being, called it "obnubilation – the conditioned habit of constantly looking in the wrong direction." Our mindset and our world-view work unconsciously and draw our attention to the things that confirm our present belief system and filter out what is contrary to it.

Early in the 20th century the French philosopher Henri Bergson discovered this phenomenon. We are constantly bombarded with an overwhelming mass of sensory input, Bergson found, and we need to pre-process these perceptions before they rise to conscious awareness. He realized that if all of our sensory input needed conscious attention, we would be overwhelmed. So, the unconscious thought processes filter out everything but the information that would be useful.

This is a little-recognized peculiarity of the way the mind works. It is an automatic reflex which we don't even notice. It's a little like the way a frog's vision works. Frogs only see things that are moving in relation to themselves, such as bugs or predators. They see only the things that are important in maintaining their self-preservation. In fact, when they flick their tongue out to catch a bug, the sensory perception of the bug and the tongue response doesn't even go through their brain: it is pure reflex.

For us, only the things that are important to the affirmation and preservation of our belief system seem to catch our attention. And our world model, which includes our belief system, is built entirely around our assumed concept of an objectified self. The mind seems to not notice or to discount the things that are contrary to our belief system, even though they may be obvious, and to only notice the things that affirm that belief system (even if it sometimes has to distort them). And we don't even realize this is occurring because most of it is happening far below the conscious level.

In fact, it is happening at this moment. Right now your mind is probably rejecting these ideas and believing that you really are quite open-minded. Indeed, you may truly feel you are even more open-minded than most people. But, then, everyone does. It is only because we can see their blind spots much more easily than our own because of the peculiar way the mind pre-processes our perceptions below the surface. And being intelligent and well-educated does not make one immune to this.

More than that, once the mind has constructed a world-view, it does everything it can to maintain it, even going so far as to distort the facts to protect the belief system from being wrong. This kind of "self-image preservation" can even be stronger than the natural instinct of physical self-preservation. This is because our belief system becomes part of our self-concept, our very identity, and the mind will do just about anything it has to do to preserve this illusory self and the belief system which sustains it. Politics and religion are prime examples of this. We assume we have excellent judgment and find it hard to understand how others could be so blind, even stupid, not to see what is obvious to us. This is mindset and it is very powerful.

Here is something you might want to try. The next time you have a disagreement with someone, try to see this process at work. You will probably forget to do this in the heat of emotion, but that's mindset too. Later, though, when you are going over it in your mind, you may remember to re-examine the situation in this light. It is easy to see others' mindset but it is almost impossible to see our own. Our "self-image preservation instinct" automatically justifies our position.

At least try to see that both of you are seeing the same thing in two different ways. Even though, to you, their way overlooks important facts. Each of you is honestly convinced your own version is the most real and factual. Mindset usually won't allow us to even consider something it perceives as a threat to it's belief system. And we don't even realize we are rejecting it. It is as though it were invisible.

Our mindset is the jailer and our world-view is the jail. But you can't break out of this prison by attacking them directly. In fact, you don't even need to attack them at all; just be aware of them and continue to observe them. Simple attention is the way to reality, freedom and rest. Under continual observation your illusions will expose themselves and simply dissolve away like the Wicked Witch of the West.

Another reason it is so very hard to examine our basic assumptions is that we don't even realize they are assumptions. We have built so much upon our basic convictions about who we are and what the world is that we never even think to question them. While we're worrying about the fine details at the top of the heap of our world-view, we never think to take a look at what they have been built upon way down on the bottom. For the foundation most greatly affects how the rest of the structure grows.

Our basic world model, the one we are using right now, was mostly built when we were less than two years old. We hadn't had much experience then, so, for the most part, we learned it from others. Studies have shown that children usually learned to identify themselves with their bodies at around the age of 17 months. That is the beginning of the self-concept. That is the foundation our belief system is built upon.

## *The Secret Entrance To A Higher Realm*

In authentic spiritual practice, attention is the means to the higher dimensions of life, and the actuality of spiritual seeking. For example, we use many important concepts and words like "self," "spirit," "soul" and "consciousness," but we don't really know what they mean. Just because we have labeled something doesn't mean we actually understand it or that it even exists. Labels give us the illusion that we know what we are talking about and, even worse, the illusion that what we are talking about is real. To begin to question these terms may make us uncomfortable at first, but this is the way to identify and reveal the concepts that perpetuate these blinding illusions that are hiding the reality.

For instance, we use the word "consciousness," but we don't really know what it is. When we use the word "consciousness" we usually intend it to mean what we are conscious *of,* i.e., the content of consciousness. Yet, at the same time, we also think consciousness is some thing or quality we *have.* But, then, we don't even know what the "we" is who has this consciousness, let alone what consciousness itself is. How muddled and contradictory we discover our beliefs are when we examine these things closely. But if we continue to exercise simple attention towards our inner processes, this confusion will dissipate. We probably never ask ourselves: "What is this that *knows* what is appearing?" Or: "What is it that knows this moment?"

Don't feel you are losing ground if a lot of these kinds of confusions pop up. This is just what you want. It is like filling a big bucket with water and a lot of leaves and papers float to the top. All of it was already there lying on the bottom, nothing is new. But now that it has risen to the top you can easily see it and take care of it. This kind of attention will reveal hidden contradictions that protect the illusions. The sooner we can be aware of them, the sooner we will be free of them.

By observing and thus exposing these empty labels that perpetuate our illusions, we will break free of them. It may be scary and confusing at first because we think those empty labels are necessary for our security. But it is just the opposite. They are the cause of all our insecurities. And they will ultimately give way because we secretly know they are empty.

The purpose of this book is not to sell you my own ideas or even to teach you anything, but to assist and guide you to closely, carefully and deeply look and observe, as I did, what actually *is* here-and-now.

You must see this for yourself and make up your own mind about what you discover and what it means to you. That is the only way it works. We may think we already know what we are and that we don't need to do this, that it would be a waste of time and effort, and that the here-and-now is boring anyway. That is very deceptive. That is mindset trying to avoid seeing something threatening, something it suspects deep down, but doesn't want to have to admit. We have an unconscious suspicion that our "self" is an empty illusion but, after all, that is better than nothing, isn't it? Except that an illusion *is* nothing.

Unfortunately, we do everything we can to avoid the here-and-now. Our mind has become addicted to distraction. It is a way of diverting our attention from our here-and-now. In truth, we fear the present moment. It is a threat to our illusory self and to our muddled and contradictory mindset. Without distractions we become very uncomfortable, so we are always looking to the future or recalling the past to avoid the here-and-now.

It doesn't take much detached self-observation to discover that we never really live in the here-and-now, but live in our *concepts* of it. We live in our imaginations of the future and our memories of the past, and in the fantasy conversations constantly going on in our mind. If you will just take a look, you will notice that you're probably doing this right now as you read this book.

The here-and-now is where you will find the secret entrance to a higher realm where few have entered before you. It takes a change in the way the mind actually operates to perceive this new reality, but it really does exist, as you will soon be experiencing for yourself.

If you will honestly, fearlessly and openly investigate, experientially, this "here-and-now," I guarantee that your discoveries will astonish you. This is truly unexplored territory, yet you will come to recognize it as your long-lost home, finally arriving where you have always been.

### The First Insight

One day I was sitting in my living room pondering about *what* I am. I remember I was looking at the bookcase. I had been reading a book about having a true self and a false self, and was trying to understand how I could have two selves. Then I began wondering who it was who had the two selves. It would take a third self to be the "me" that had them. I think that must have locked up my mind for a moment. For just an instant I didn't seem to be able to think about anything. I was just looking at the bookcase but not seeing anything, not thinking anything. That's when the answer came. It was so clear and so obvious. The self I thought I was, was just that, a thought. *That* was what the false self was.

Now, even though that first insight was mostly intellectual, it still had a great deal of impact. I felt it emotionally and it was very liberating. I began to feel relief and joy immediately.

I can remember at the time wondering momentarily what the True Self was. I had seen what I was *not*, but not what I *was*. But the sheer relief of realizing that I no longer had to live in bondage to a mere concept overshadowed everything. Soon after, I found the passage in the Bible where it said: "He ... was the light that lighteth every man that cometh into the World." (John 1:9) I knew I was on to something.

At that time I had no understanding of non-duality so I could not help but think of the True Self in terms of an individual, objective entity.

However, that approach did take me quite a ways. And I ended up writing a book about it called *The Present Kingdome of God*. Yet, even before I had finished writing that book, I had actually begun the next step.

Some time later I was in a strange little bookstore that carried all kinds of religious, philosophical and spiritual books. A thin little book on the top shelf caught my eye. I took it down, opened it somewhere in the middle and read a paragraph at random. I was astounded by what I read. Here was everything I had been trying so hard to understand! The book was called *All Else Is Bondage, Non-Volitional Living,* and the author's name was Wei Wu Wei. Not only was he talking about what I had discovered earlier, but he also posited that we could not be *any entity* or *any thing.* He was a scholar and used a lot of words that I wasn't very familiar with and the book was kind of hard to follow. But I see now that that was good because I had attached conditioned meanings to most of the religious and philosophical terms I was familiar with, meanings that were part of my mindset. The unfamiliar words he used were very precise and helped me to understand things with fewer preconceived notions getting in the way.

I didn't know at the time that Wei Wu Wei was the pen name of Terence Gray. Later I was able to acquire his address from Paul Reps, the author of *Zen Flesh, Zen Bones,* when he gave a local workshop. The funny thing was, I had found Terence Gray's name in the copyright line of another book of his called *Posthumous Pieces,* and because of the word "Posthumous" in the title I thought: "Great. I've finally found someone who can help me and now I find out he is dead." But Paul Reps assured me that Terence Gray was very much alive and well, that he was a friend of his and, in fact, he had just visited him not long ago. This led to a correspondence with Terence Gray whose patience, kindness and books ultimately led to a life-inspiring insight.

*"Man seeks his inward unity,
but his real progress on the path
depends upon his capacity to refrain from
distorting reality in accordance with his desires."*
—Goethe

Now, do Reality Meditation # 2 once again.

# IN A NUTSHELL
## *Reality Meditation # 3*
## Fasting Of The Mind

First, give yourself permission to not have to accomplish anything for the next hour. The idea that you must gain something or accomplish something with this meditation will get in the way of just doing it and will put the mind in the improper attitude.

This meditation is to open the mind to non-linear, non-dual, intuitive awareness.

Sit upright, hands on your lap, feet on the floor. Wear comfortable clothes. Pick an uninteresting spot somewhere in front of you at which to direct your gaze, then let your eyes go out of focus. Keeping the eyes open is simply to help keep you from falling asleep.

Focus the mind on the wordless sense of awareness. (Other ways to say it would be the tacit sense of "am-ness," or the sense of consciousness, or awareness of awareness, or *this* which knows this moment.) Then still the mind by ignoring any thoughts which may arise.

What we call thinking is mostly three mental activities: sub-vocalization, images and emotions. Thoughts can't actually be purposely stopped because they are an automatic reflex. However you can continually draw focus away from thoughts, you can diminish them and open yourself to a cessation of thoughts. Each time a word, image or emotion begins to form, turn your attention away from it and ignore it. Or as Nisargadatta said: "look over its shoulders."

At first this may take great effort, not only to continually dismiss thoughts, but to keep doing the meditation. The mind is uncomfortable doing this and will bring up all sorts of distractions. But it will get easier the more you do it.

This way of meditating may not seem to be important and, indeed, just boring, but persist. You will begin to recognize this clear consciousness as the source and substance, the ground of all that appears, from your closest thoughts to the furthest stars. This is what-you-are, perfectly clear and still. You will begin to see the world in a new, higher, miraculous way.

This practice goes against your conditioned need for distraction and your habit of talking to yourself in thoughts. That is why it may be difficult at first. You may have to start with just five minutes and add a few minutes each day to build up to an hour. By stilling linear thought (not talking to yourself by ignoring it) and focusing on the tacit sense of consciousness, you are allowing deeper non-linear, intuitive understanding to rise to the surface of consciousness. But it will not appear in thoughts. Don't look for anything to happen. It will appear as an inner understanding of the nature of reality. Later, you will find that it is suddenly "just there." However, at the same time you are making the mind available to a full awakening experience.

## In A Nutshell

This chapter focuses on the heart of Non-Volitional Living. Later chapters will clarify and expand upon this basic foundation.

Why are we so unhappy? Because not everything goes our way. Because we dread doing the things we don't want to do, but have to do. And we can't do many of the things we want to do. All this boils down to the fact that we feel we are a person with desires and needs that conflict with our circumstances and our responsibilities. In other words our "volition" is not always in line with what is happening or what should be done. An understanding of what-we-are and what the mind is can free us from this false sense of volition and remove the burden of our responsibilities. Then, we actually will be happy, and without even trying.

### You Are Not The Mind

We have been taught that the mind is our self, thinking.

We cannot be the mind because we are what is perceiving the mind. Look for yourself right now. You are looking at thoughts from a higher, prior level. But we cannot perceive our self just as our eye cannot see itself, because it is what is looking. The mind cannot be our self. The Chinese Ch'an master Hsi Yün (Huang Po) said: "A perception cannot perceive." So, are you the perceptions (thoughts and feelings) of a "me" or what is perceiving them?

We feel we are the mind because of the way the mind itself works. The mind understands things by comparing perceptions and creating objective concepts of them so it can compare one concept with another. This is dualistic, intellectual knowledge, and it soon creates a concept of itself as "me" and there the trouble begins. Thus, the mind associates the sense of "me" with it's operation and with the body, and we believe and feel we are an individual, thinking, acting entity. This is the origin of all our suffering. Once we feel we are an individual we begin to see and evaluate everything as it relates to us as an individual. We become a thing in a universe of things. A very small, vulnerable, but supremely important (at least to ourselves) individual, in a vast, infinite, seemingly purposeless, uncaring cosmos. We lose our original, true sense of identity with the Absolute.

### The Mind Goes Its Own Way

By watching our thoughts over a period of time, we can see that the mind is operating literally by itself. Thoughts just appear and keep on appearing automatically. We have this feeling that it is "me" who is thinking, but this feeling is just a conditioned reflex caused by the concept of our self as an individual. By watching thoughts we can see how they appear unbidden and un-owned, as a bird in the sky. Just try not thinking for even a few seconds and see that it is impossible. You will think about not thinking. There is no "me" controlling these thoughts. We may have the illusion of purposely thinking about a particular subject, but notice that the idea to purposely think about something comes by itself. Then we do it, automatically, but with the false feeling we are the "decider." That feeling of being the "decider" is not us, it belongs to the mind. It is something we are perceiving.

It will take more than just a few minutes of thought-watching to prove this definitively. It often takes many months of diligent watching to really see it and to be convinced. This is because the conditioned feeling of being the thinker is so deep that the very idea that the mind goes its own way seems ridiculous. But the payoff of this single discovery is enormous in terms of liberation and deeper understanding of ourselves and the universe.

The very idea that the mind is operating by itself is unacceptable for most people because it seems to remove the control of the mind from the individual, and allows the individual to cease accepting responsibility for his actions.

This is a valid reason from the point of view of an "individual." Because the mind conceives of itself as an individual, it uses this fear of harm to itself or reward for itself as a form of inhibition to keep from doing things that would be "wrong" (ultimately harmful to it or to its image of itself). However, this is not you; it is the mind regulating itself. This is where feelings of bondage and frustration come from.

The best control is to see that you don't need control at all. Because the mind conceives of itself as an individual, it accumulates conflicting needs and desires. The purpose is not just to release the inhibitions that keep us under control, but to dissolve the mind's illusion of itself as an individual in charge of, and identified with, the mind. That will, at the same time, begin to dissolve the inhibitions as well as the need for them because the conflicting needs and desires will disappear with the illusory self.

### You Are Not The Doer

You have never "done" anything. Because the mind has conceived itself to be an individual it conceives of itself as the "thinker" and also the "actor" or "doer." Yet it is not anyone. The mind is not a thing or an entity but a *process*, the thinking process. It is simply a process that is happening automatically, in the same way that the heart is beating automatically.

This is why we cannot live the perfect life, even though we have been taught how a "good" person should act. We know we shouldn't get angry at those we love, but despite the greatest resolve, we still do. Why? Because they are not *our* thoughts or *our* actions, because we are not the thinker of our thoughts nor the doer of our actions. We are not even the experiencer of the experience. What are we? We are what is perceiving the mind and that is not a person.

We are what is perceiving the doing, but we are not the doer. We never were. We have never done the bad things and we have never done the good things either. Thoughts are affected by the environment (such as the words in this book), inner habits and tendencies, and by the mind's concept of a "me," but not by any "actual" me. We are incapable of interfering with the mind. Why? Because there is no one to interfere. We aren't anyone. Thus, we absolutely cannot have any volition. The concept of being an individual is an invention of the mind itself. It is an artifact of the way the mind works. The feeling of volition is an illusion spawned by this concept of a "me."

We can never find our own will (volition) in any action. Every so-called action is actually an automatic reaction of the mind with an accompanying feeling of volition. It is not "me," it is the mind automatically going its own way. Simply watch the mind. Focus on how it is operating. Be aware of it. That's all that can be done. That is all we can *ever* do. That is all we have ever done. It is the mind that thinks and feels otherwise and we are what is *aware* of what the mind thinks and feels. We are perfectly open, empty and still. We are not in space or time. We can never be affected in any way. We have no needs or desires whatever. We just shine brilliantly, effortlessly.

We are what perceives what is appearing. In fact, it is because of this perceiving that anything at all appears. What we are is the being-ness of what appears. The is-ness, or the am-ness, if you will, of the very sense of "I am." Another way to put it is that we are the Awareness in which everything appears – the here-now, the sense of presence, consciousness.

See that we are simply and only the awareness of the mind while it goes its own way. Every sensation and feeling it has belongs to the mind, to manifestation, not to our self. With everything that appears in any way, we can say: "Not me, not me."

We are the watching, not the thinker, or the doer, or the experiencer. Once this is deeply and completely understood, the mind can let go of its sense of volition and its sense of being an individual, relax and just be. Everything happens by itself. Everything happens as it should. Everything happens as it must.

When the mind lets go of its sense of self and volition there is the deepest sense of complete peace and fulfillment. It is the Bliss spoken of by the ancient masters. All fear disappears.

We are now looking from our True Source (as we always were but didn't realize) the timeless, spaceless, Absolute, the Unmanifest. This is what we all are. This is the ultimate source of our light of awareness. We are perceiving the manifest *from* its source, the unmanifest, and it unfolds spatially and temporally as it eternally IS.

## *One Giant Leap For Mankind...*

I wrote the preceding section as an article in 1993 under the title *An Exploration of Non-Volitional Living,* and it has been available on the internet for several years. I originally wrote it just for myself because I wanted to see how succinctly I could express my understanding. I sent it to a friend just to share it with him and he put it on his web site. However, it is necessarily expressed in dualistic terms and, as I have been reminded, the problem is that some readers may still imagine themselves as someone or some "thing" doing the watching, such as a "watcher."

The action of watching, staying focused on Pure Consciousness and disidentification with the perceived *can* lead to Awakening, but *dualism* is the real problem. And it should be the next issue we address.

When I was trying to understand the non-dual, it seemed so mysterious, as if it required some kind of giant leap of understanding to see. But, thanks again to Terence Gray, I saw it really takes only a small step.

Writing under the name of Wei Wu Wei, he expressed it wonderfully in his powerful little book, *All Else is Bondage, Non-Volitional Living*, originally published in 1964 by Hong Kong

University Press. On page 41, *The Living Dream*, Mr. Gray talks about entering a restaurant where you *see* a table, *hear* people talking, *taste* what you are eating, *smell* the wine in your glass, *feel* the knife and fork in your hands, and you *know* that you are having lunch. Then, Mr. Gray states that none of this actually happens as a series of external events experienced by you. Why so?

While all of this does appear in consciousness, the seer and the seen are actually conceptualized, (objectified, using space and time), from only the see-ing: the hearer and the heard are conceptualized from the hear-ing: the taster and the tasted are conceptualized from the taste-ing: the smeller and the smelled are conceptualized from the smell-ing, and the feeler and the felt are conceptualized from the feel-ing. The apparent seer and seen, hearer and heard, taster and tasted, smeller and smelled, feeler and felt, do not exist as things-in-themselves, but are all objectified (interpreted as objects) by the dualistic thought process from see-ing, hear-ing, taste-ing, smell-ing and touch-ing, which themselves, are all simply a perceiv-ing.

This may be even easier to understand when we see how we do this objectifying in a sleeping dream. During a dream we believe that it is real, that we are an apparent seer – "me" – see-ing the seen, and so on for the other senses. Yet, when we awaken, we see that both our apparent "self" and the apparent "others" were only interpreted by the mind as separate, individual objects and apparent entities. They were not really objects or things-in-themselves. They took up no space in our bedroom while we were dreaming them, they were all just the phenomenon of dream-ing. In fact, the highest of the great masters have been telling us throughout history that this "reality," where we think we are awake, and we think we are a separate individual in an infinite pre-existing universe, is also created in the same way. This is the "living dream," they tell us, and it, also, is all created by the phenomenon of perceiv-ing, in consciousness.

It may be easier to see that the dreamed "others" weren't real individuals than it is for us to see that our dreamed "self" is not really us either, for when we awaken we seem to still be here while the "others" and the whole dreamed world are gone. Yet, if we just look at perceiv-ing, and understand how the mind is taking this *process* of perceiv-ing and interpreting it, or dividing it as two apparent "things,"[2] a perceiver and a perceived, we can see that the dreamed self, as the perceiver, did not actually exist as a thing-in-itself, an object or an independent entity. Our "self" was a dreamed concept as were the "others." If we can see that, then, quite possibly, we can also see that the "self" we think we are right here and now is just as much a fiction. There is no seer and no seen, just see-ing

---

2. The ancient masters called it split-mind.

objectified conceptually as seer and seen. And you can do this with any or all of the other senses.

Who then is dreaming this "living dream?"

No one, of course. There never has been a dreamer. For haven't we just seen how a perceiving is being automatically conceptualized as perceiver and perceived? Dreaming is conceived to exist as an apparent dreamer and a dream, but ironically, by analyzing the dream process itself we can see that there is only the dream-ing. There are no such "things" as a dreamer or a dream. In the living dream there is only the perceiv-ing. There are no actual entities or things and never have been.

Reality, then, is actually non-dual. It just *seems* to be dualistic because of the way the thought process works. This can be recognized by seeing that most basic concepts are invented by the neat trick of grouping perceptions into mutually-exclusive, interdependent opposites and then assuming them to be things-in-themselves (such as "up" and "down"). While each opposite excludes the other by its nature, at the same time each depends on its opposite to give it meaning.

This is the "Great Secret" that no one suspects. And, for most people, even if suggested or understood at all, is instantly dismissed and almost never taken seriously. It is not a secret because it is being hidden, but because the mind has a conditioned habit of thinking only in terms of apparent objects such as "perceiver" and "perceived," and is not accustomed to recognizing both as actually one perceiv-ing. We can't even imagine not being a "self."

But "self" is an interdependent concept whose opposite is "other" or "not-self." Neither can exist without the other. The concept "self" depends on the concept "other" to give it meaning by exclusion. "Other" depends on "self" to give it meaning by exclusion. They are interdependent and at the same time mutually-exclusive.

Many, at first, will consciously or uncon-sciously (because of mindset) interpret non-volitional living as a kind of fatalism. It is not, be-cause there is no "me" to be at the mercy of fate. But there can be no halfway with this. If one believes in a "me" that has no volition, that is worse than no understanding at all and will lead to apathy, license and depression. Or, if one believes in volition, but no self, this will cause similar problems. Both misunderstandings are obvious contradictions.

In the proper understanding of non-volition lies complete freedom with proper action. Non-volition is neither doing nor not-doing. The seeming loss of volition and self will stop many right at the start and they will never see past that. In truth this is their prison. We cannot lose what we have never had. Right understanding is our real liberation.

Objectivizing is not wrong in itself, it's just that when the thought process objectifies its self (in thought) as an independent entity, and *then identifies with this imaginary entity as who it is*, it causes all kinds of trouble. It is responsible for all our bondage and suffering, because we then see our objects as "other than ourselves" instead of as aspects of what-we-are. And an independent entity, "me" can have unpleasant things happen to it. If you are not a self, then what can happen to you? However, as long as you are identified with a volitional self you must judge yourself as one and be held accountable.

Earlier in this section was the quote by Terence Gray: "and you *know* you are having lunch." We have just seen that there is neither the knower nor the known, but there is a know-ing. And herein lies the heart of the matter. We *know* that we are having lunch or whatever we are doing. Right now you know you are reading a book. My computer doesn't know that it is computing, but I know that I am writing. I know that "I am," though not as any "one" or as any "thing," and this *know-ing that I know* is a great miracle. It can only be recognized by looking here, now. This is what I am, and what you are. This is what-we-are. And this is the Source of the dream-ing of the living dream. You see, the non-dual reality is really so very simple. No perceiver nor perceived, just the phenomenon of perceiv-ing. And this is what *you* are. This is what *everything* is. Just as in the sleeping dream, everything in the dream existed only in and as the phenomenon of dream-ing. Once this is recognized, so many other questions will be answered.

This is called "Awakening" or whole-mind.

There is more about the amazing implications of the "living dream" and how it is supported by quantum physics in further chapters. But before we end this chapter, let's take one more look at the Nisargadatta quote at the beginning...

*"Nothing perceived can be me or mine."*

When we first read that powerful quote from Nisargadatta, the thought processes usually overlook the fact that this doesn't just mean automobiles, buildings, other people, etc., cannot be me. It also means "your" own body, your thoughts, your mind, your emotions, your desires, your understanding and knowledge, your decisions, your actions, your personality, your goodness, your badness – *anything* perceived in any way. Get the idea? If you think you have it or think you perceive it, it's not you or yours.

But, you say: "I'm left with nothing!" Exactly![3] Until it is apparent that nothing can be you or yours, you won't be able to see that, phenomenally speaking, you are *everything*. But again, that is still not anything. Rather, it is neither something nor nothing. It is the interdependent concepts of both something and nothing that appear in consciousness. It is all percepts spontaneously arising in noumenal consciousness via temporal extension. You must come to see that you are Pure Consciousness – that is, consciousness without

---

3. The Ch'an Masters would not be as approving. They would demand, "Throw the nothing out too!"

content. Yet, even consciousness will eventually dissolve into the Absolute.

Ninety nine percent of the questions I am asked wouldn't be asked if it were realized that "nothing perceived" means any and *all mental content* (as well as the body). There is nothing to be done. You don't have to get rid of or stop anything to awaken. It can happen in a moment when it is recognized that "nothing perceived" means *everything* percieved, both "inner" and "outer." Nisargadatta is just stating the obvious, that anything you see (perceive physically or mentally) couldn't be you or yours because it has to be apart from you (mentally objectified) to be seen, just as you obviously don't mistake a person on the street for yourself because they are someone you can see "over there" and you are here where you are looking *from*. If you were that person, you would be looking from over there where he is and you couldn't see him, because that would be where you are looking *from*. Of course this also holds true for whatever is perceived mentally as well.

### Taken By Surprise During The Fasting Of The Mind

Many years ago, I had been doing the "Fasting of the Mind" as detailed at the beginning of this chapter as much as possible for two or three weeks solid. I was working at home at the time and was able to devote a good part of the day to it. When I had a task to do, I just did it and returned to the fasting as soon as possible.

One Sunday afternoon, the house was quiet and I was sitting on the couch "fasting." I had become so accustomed to doing it every spare moment that I truly had forgotten about any benefits or even any reason for doing it. So I was not trying to accomplish anything or to have any experience.

We have a clock on the mantle which ticks very loudly. Without attempting to, and I don't know how it happened, I begin to feel the ticks within my body, and then I *was* the ticking. Even my heartbeat was synchronized with the ticking of the clock.

Just then I felt my "self" actually, physically, plunge downward with great force. The thought came: "I just am." The thought was not *my* thought but just *a* thought. The ancient Ch'an Masters described this as being like the bottom falling out of a bucket of water you are carrying, and that is just how it was. I'm describing this in words and thoughts, but at the time there were no words or thoughts happening, just the naked sense that "I just am." I was not apart from it but had no intellectual or volitional part in it. It just happened spontaneously.

When the self fell away, all that was left was what I can only described as "am-ness." I was not anyone or anything. I was obviously, clearly just the am-ness of all, the being and actuality of all, and all was just as it should be. This didn't mean that everything was the way the mind would like it to be or that the mind's desired ideals were fulfilled or unfolded according to the mind's concepts of good and evil. Things are always as they should be according to our True Being or our "Real Self" – as they *must* be at this moment. This is harmony with the universe.

An imperfect analogy would be something like a play or movie, where everyone was playing their part perfectly. Some were "good" and some were "bad," but that was how the story was supposed to go.

There was an overwhelming sense of total completion and total fulfillment. This sense of total completion permeated the entire universe. I felt that this must be the "bliss" spoken of in eastern philosophy as well as the "peace that passes understanding" in the Bible. However, it is not a feeling, it just *is*.

Then, a few moments later, time and space dissolved. And with it, all phenomenality, all perceptions, everything that was appearing. That, too, was "as it should be."

When space and time dissolved, the only way to articulate it is that, in one timeless moment, I was *everyone and everything* that ever was and is and will be. All this was actually lived in less than an instant. On later reflection I understood it was what we call eternity, and this is my (our) very being.

I must assume this experience is what some have called "Universal Consciousness" or "Cosmic Consciousness" or "God" or just "the All." This was far more "real" than what we experience as everyday waking reality. My True Being was actually God's being – not just a *part* of it, but *all* of it. As an individual self, I was not God. There was no individual self, but only God, appearing as what-we-are.

This was not a vision nor even a new state of mind. It was just what is when the mental processes stopped over-interpreting the raw phenomenal perceptions and just let go of its imagined need to control the mental processes.

The next thing that happened was that this Universal Consciousness also dissolved. However, there is no way to even indicate in any way what was "upstream" of the Universal Consciousness. There is no way to express this.

Afterward, I could only assume that this is what has been referred to by the great Ch'an and Vedanta Masters as the "Absolute," which is ultimately what we all are as our noumenal, original aspect. This might be conceptualized as "upstream" or beyond Pure Consciousness, but to make any kind of concept about this is grossly misleading. It can only be a condescension to indicate "it" with any word as it cannot ever be an "it."

This experience then reversed itself, and as time and space returned, so did phenomenality and the thought came of itself to "just be." This "re-entry" carried the understanding that being what-we-are is the easiest thing in the world because it is spontaneous. It happens by itself. It is absolute rest. This is all we ever have to "do" or can do. Yet, even that happens by itself when the mind lets go. The sense of total completion, total fulfillment was still there.

The only problem with "just being" is that, ordinarily, the mind won't cooperate and must assert the sense of volition as it operates. It can only lose this habit and "let go" as understanding penetrates and dissolves this illusion. This, in essence, is really the only thing obscuring our actuality, our absolute rest and total liberation.

Now, do Reality Meditation #3 once again.

# WHAT IS A WORLD MODEL?

## *Reality Meditation # 4*
## The "Hand" Experiment

We will now discover visually what-we-are, the same way we have recognized it mentally.

First, hold your right hand out in front of your face. Do this now.

Look at the back of your hand. Notice that it has color, shape, size, etc.

Notice the lines on the back of your hand, your fingernails, the space between your fingers.

Now, continue to look straight ahead and move your hand slowly to the right and back past the right side of your head. You may move your eyes to watch your hand, but not your head. Keep moving your hand in that direction slowly until it disappears completely from view. Then move it forward and toward the left until it appears again.

Now, move it in and out of this "area." Can you actually see where it goes when it disappears?

*Do not imagine or conceive of where it goes.* You are only to go by your present visual perceptions. Does it go into something? Does it go into a black hole of nothing?

Or does it disappear into neither something nor nothing? This is no-thingness.

Does this "area" that your hand goes into have any color or shape?

Is it black and large or white and tiny?

Can it be thought of or visualized at all?

This is actually the "light" that makes all light shine – "the light that lighteth every man that cometh into the World."

It cannot be seen itself as anything, but is the Source and substance of all that appears. It is ultimately and really what-you-are.

Up to now you have thought you were only one side of the dualism of self/other, but now you can see (in-see) and identify with the underlying Source of both. This Source – Light, Spirit, Consciousness – is ineffable, nothing you can really describe conceptually or visually, neither something nor nothing, neither object nor space. You could say that it is absolutely pure and absolutely still. Here, at the Source it is absolutely empty: "out there," as perceptions, it is absolutely full.

Do not be fooled by its simplicity and nearness. Do not be fooled by finding "the light of the world," present here and now (where you thought your head was), instead of finding it in a complicated set of abstract, theological ideas.

Every perception of color, movement, object or space appears "out there."

The absolutely empty, still, clear, spotless Source of those perceptions is *here.*

NOTE: Your feelings, thoughts and actions are also interdependent opposites (happy/sad) and are always attached to phenomenality – things and objects. That is where they belong, with the world of things "out there."[4]

What you have just discovered is upstream of, or prior to, feelings, thoughts, actions, things or anything objective whatsoever. But to appear at all, it must appear as "other" than it really is. It appears then as "the (total) world," whether it be thoughts, feelings, mountains or stars.

What you really are, their Source *here,* is always empty, pure and still. It must be or it would obscure what is appearing. It is the peace that passes understanding. Notice also that there is nothing such as a "self" *here* either. No "self" or no "other" *here.* No objective entity at all, just no-thingness.

Yet, this is the Source in which all concepts and perceptions appear.

-----

4. Unless you have chronic depression and/or an organic imbalance of neurotransmitters and neurons. In that case feelings such as sadness may not be attached to an object. Still, it is not you or yours.

In recognizing that you are no-thing you have become everything. This is losing your life to find it. It is "thick darkness" to split-mind, yet "the light" to whole-mind.

It is really what-you-are, as you are.

You have finally returned home.

## *What Is A World Model?*

*"I see nobody on the road," said Alice.*

*"I only wish I had such eyes," the king remarked in a fretful tone.*

*"To be able to see nobody! And at that distance too!*

*Why, it's as much as I can do to see real people, by this light!"*

*–Lewis Carroll*

*Through the Looking-Glass*

We assume that our perceptions are a direct awareness of what is really "out there" in the world. It seems self-evident and all too obvious that the senses are simply channels for information coming from the outside world.

Common sense tells us this, but common sense would also tell us that the sun moves and the earth stands still. But we know the earth revolves around the sun. (Let's not be like the men who refused to look into Galileo's telescope.) In a similar manner, this Newtonian world we perceive is not at all like the world physicists describe. Having grown up with the idea of a real world "out there" it is next to impossible to doubt it. This is because we create "out there" and "in here" conceptually. But before we tackle that, let's first try to understand just why we see the world as we do.

In the nineteenth century, a number of interesting things were discovered about perception, but were largely forgotten until the computer was invented and scientists began trying to get their computers to do some of the same things we humans do. After all, they thought, isn't the brain just a computer too? They assumed it must simply be processing the sensory nervous signals which are being stimulated by the environment to discover what is "out there."

In his fascinating book on perception, *A Second Way of Knowing,* author Edmund Bolles reports how scientists believed that they could get a computer to see by analyzing the output from a video camera to tell what it was pointed at. They thought they could simply store, in an index, a lot of rules about how things looked and, by comparing this with what was on the screen, the computer could "understand" what is out there.

The task proved to be far more difficult than that. The scientists have had to realize that it takes something far more sophisticated than the quantitative analysis of the signals from the camera to understand what the camera is "seeing," and that humans must see in an entirely different way than had been assumed.

## People Are Not Computers

The stimulus from "out there" is interpreted "in here" according to our world model. Our world model is our understanding of what phenomenality (the world) is and how it works. From the moment we are born we begin to try to understand what our five senses are telling us. We begin to form reflexes, then ideas, then a model of what they all mean together. As we begin to be able to communicate with others, we get ideas from them about what we are and what the world is. The way our bodies and minds work also affects how we form our world model.

For example, we would assume that the eye sees the seven primary colors and sends the information via wavelengths to the brain. But Bolles describes how experiments have shown that the eye responds best to just three parts of the electromagnetic spectrum: violet at 419 nanometers, green at 531 nanometers and yellow-green at 558 nanometers. It responds to a far lesser degree to the rest of the visible spectrum. The eye computes all the colors we perceive from these responses and transmits a qualitative (subjective) description of the color we are aware of. We call this the "visible" part of the electromagnetic spectrum, not because it has some quality that makes it visible, but because that is the part that the eye responds to. The eye could just as well have responded to a much larger portion. "Then," as Bolles remarks," we could be seeing radio and television waves."

Science knows only wavelengths, yet we see color – a purely *subjective* experience of perception. Oddly enough, an object absorbs most of the color wavelengths but reflects the wave lengths we see, so we are actually seeing it as the one color that it isn't.

The Materialists or realists insist that everything we perceive is "out there" in the environment. But, actually, "out there" is a subjective construct, even though we don't feel like we are "constructing" our reality. We feel confident that we are just observing it as it is. But science interprets the world quantitatively with mechanical knowledge. We "see" using *qualitative* knowledge. In other words, we see by *perceptual meanings*.

Perceptual meanings are *the subjective experience of knowing*. A computer "knows" a lot with its stored data, but it doesn't *know* that it knows. Television sets do not *know* that images are on their screens. Consciousness is *knowing* that one knows something. Science cannot understand this kind of knowing which is so fundamental to our daily life.

A telephone works by turning sound vibration into electrical signals which are a form of mechanical information or code for the vibrations. At the other end the electrical signals are turned back into sound. These signals can be measured, recorded and interpreted by other devices. However, sensory nerves operate to create sensations, not mechanical information. Our senses interpret the world qualitatively according to its subjective meaning. Science has no way of understanding this, since there can be no mechanical, quantitative way to measure percepts. In fact, science has no idea what perceptions are and prefers to ignore the subject altogether. They recognize the act of perception, but they cannot quantify them or even verify that we share the same subjective perceptions. And since science works by measurement or quantification, they are forced to ignore them.

"Science doesn't know why perceptions exist or how they work or why the world appears so steady. What we see remains more consistent than reality," says Bolles. In a photo most coins and wheels are actually ovals. Yet we mentally "see" a coin or wheel as round, no matter what angle we see it from because we *know* it is round. In a photo, people are not the same size, the ones nearer to the camera are bigger. Nevertheless we *know* people are much the same size because we *know* that they don't really get smaller as they walk away. In other words, we readjust the optical illusion of them appearing to be different sizes because our minds "know" about perspective and distance. In fact, there are no people or objects in any photo, just colors and shading. Any people or objects we see in a photo are constructed in the mind and mentally interpreted as people and objects. The wonder is that we do see objects in a photo. Animals rarely see figures in photos. One of the reasons animals don't often recognize figures in a photo is that they rely heavily on scent clues and without the meaningful scent data pictures don't usually catch their attention.

There are enough of these examples to fill another book, but once we realize this is happening, it's more fun to see if we can discover some of them for ourselves.

This interpretation of percepts is automatic, effortless and without thought. It happens almost instantly and we usually have no clue that it is even happening. Many creatures use this automatic interpretation to their advantage to camouflage themselves so that we may not even see them and they are misinterpreted as "background." Camouflage is used by predator and prey alike for that reason. But once in a while we are surprised by an object or creature that is unfamiliar to us and we catch ourselves trying to figure out what it might be. When we are surprised this way everything else we are doing seems to come to a screeching halt. Our body momentarily freezes, and our attention narrows down exclusively to this one strange object while we try to fit it into our world model.

## Reality Is Not "Out There"

*"When you make the two become one, and when you make the inside like the outside and the outside like the inside, and the upper like the lower...*

*then you will enter the kingdom."*

–The Gospel according to Thomas

"Inside" and "outside" are such basic interdependent concepts that we don't even realize that they are just inventions of the mind used to interpret our world model. The world we are so sure is "out there" depends on a mental construction of our own. For instance, we say that dreams don't come from "out there" but originate from "in here."

Of course, we know there is neither an actual "in here" nor an "out there" in a dream. But during the dream the "in here" (in our mind) is believed to be the "out there" (the dream world) just as this book is being interpreted as being "out there" right now. The brain is not just a symbol processor like a telephone or a computer, but a producer of sensations, of subjective experience. In fact, even what we call the brain, is itself interpreted this way. What the brain is should become clear in later chapters.

Sensations are qualities of the immeasurable experience of awareness. Actually, things are not "out there." Nor is there an "in here" where perceptions are interpreted. Percepts are dependent upon understanding. Perceptual meaning does not come from logic but by associating one kind of sensation with another.

We construct "things" mentally because of the way the mind works and the world model we have formed. The idea "tree" is not "out there." We experience sensations such as emotions and imagination, etc., which are not "out there" in our world model and are not included in the five physical senses, so we interpret them as "in here."

You may think you can simply photograph a tree and that proves it is "out there." But proving it is "out there" goes for the camera and the picture and even your own head and body too. Also, you can't photograph or record your senses of "tree," the sensual perceptions we have labeled "tree." The sound perceptions of wind blowing through the leaves, the hard, bumpy feel of the trunk, the smell of the warm sun on the bark, the subtle shades of green in the leaves, all taken together give you the qualitative here and now sensual experience of a tree. Those percepts that belong to the tree are separated from the rest of your flow of perceptions and conceptually symbolized as a separate part of it all, as a thing-in-itself.

Most of us have seen movie film and know that it is a series of still pictures. What we see as movement is actually many still pictures flashed quickly, one after the other. On a movie screen nothing actually moves. We construct the movement. It is called persistence of vision and the movement is all in the interpretation. Likewise, music and melody are constructed from sound. Music is sound but the musical melody is not part of the physical and is not measurable: it is a subjective invention. At most we can quantify music as certain similar or reoccurring data patterns. But what we know as "music to our ears" is a subjective experience.

### Our World-view Is Learned

In her book, *Pilgrim at Tinker Creek*, Annie Dillard writes about blind people who have never seen but have gained sight through a corneal transplant operation and must learn to see. They have no understanding of distance as space, only as time. They don't know what a tree is until they feel it. They don't know what shadows are. One person said that lemonade tasted "square." Some became so frustrated and confused that they had to close their eyes and return to their more familiar, more comfortable sightless world.

We see meaning, not mechanical, quantifiable reality. Meaning is also affected by language and culture. It is said that the Hopi understanding of time is very different from other cultures. We think our meaning of time is obvious and self-evident, and it is until, as Saint Augustine remarked, someone asks us what it is. "What then is time? If no one asks me, I know; if I want to explain it to someone who does ask me, I do not know."

Our perceptions create the impression of an absolute space and time – something apart from us that we move through. We take it for granted that it really is that way. But it all comes from our mental world model. Space and time are actually concepts used to "project" the phenomenal world. We construct the world by extending it in the three spatial directions and the one temporal direction as duration.

Zeno's famous paradoxes derive from the way we objectify space-time as something in itself, apart from us, instead of understanding it as consciousness' mechanism of manifestation. For example, Zeno argued that it was impossible to shoot an arrow to a target. Before the arrow could go to the target it must first go half the way. But before it could go half the way, it first must go half the way to that half-way. But before it could go that half way, it must first go half the way... and so on infinitely and, thus it could never reach the target. And yet it does.

## *The Two Levels Of Perception*

The first and primary level of perception is *sensory* knowledge – percepts. That's where we start as babies. This level is a more non-linear kind of perception. It is our intuitive, holistic level. Non-linear comprehension is where we can see the "big picture," where we, as adults, sometimes get those magnificent, timeless flashes of spiritual insight, where we suddenly see the "real meaning of life" and the simplicity and interrelatedness of all things. This is our purest, most "real" level of living.

The second level of perception is *symbolic* knowledge – concepts. This is really an artificial layer of meaning constructed of labels and concepts where we (unfortunately) spend most of our waking, thinking life. It is a linear kind of perception where our world model expresses itself in our thoughts, language and sequential communication.

One way to begin to understand the difference between linear and non-linear perception is to compare looking at a picture with reading a description of the same scene. When we look at a picture we get the sense of the whole scene immediately. This is non-linear perceiving. When we read a description of the same scene it unfolds in a linear, serial, word-by-word, progression over time.

The physical world is the "real world" only because our world model interprets it that way. But it is not the basic "material stuff" we have assumed it to be.  The new physics has proven experimentally that ours is not a world of matter, time and space as we had thought, and that there really is no "out there" nor, indeed, "in here."  The Danish physicist, Niels Bohr, said that to try to understand how quantum physics applies to our everyday reality would lead to madness.  Yet, we *must* understand because it points to a higher dimension of living.  As they used to say in the theater: "Don't be alarmed ladies and gentlemen, it's all part of the show."  Don't be alarmed readers, we shall soon see for ourselves that our reality is all part of the mental construct.

## *Why Do We Appear To Be "In The World?"*

Why are we here?  And with this psycho-somatic apparatus (mind-body)?  Why do we even need a body?  Why is there this seemingly physical system which affects the five senses of the body and is known by consciousness?

First, it only *seems* that we exist in the world because our world model interprets it that way.  Next, the only way phenomenality (a world) can manifest or can appear is from an apparent *viewpoint.*  Consciousness conceptually extends itself in the three spatial directions and in one temporal direction (as duration) to create space-time, and uses what we know as the psyche-soma (mind-body) as the viewpoint, to interact, to be and to know itself. In other words, consciousness extends spatially and temporally to appear to "itself" as "the world." This includes what our world model is interpreting as "you" and "me." Remember how we do this in the sleeping dream? It works the same way in this, the "living dream."

The realization we are aiming for is that we are not a thing apart from the rest of the world. We are not a spirit trapped in a body. We are no-one and no-thing (noumenally) and thus, we are everyone and everything (phenomenally).

We will have more fun with the illusion of "things" and the new physics in later chapters.

Now, do Reality Meditation #4 once again.

# A DISILLUSIONING EXPERIENCE

*Reality Meditation # 5*

## Is Consciousness In Your Body?

We don't realize how deep our learned assumptions are embedded. Could all this really be a projection of consciousness? Is it really just a matter of how it has been interpreted? Dare we recognize that consciousness is not some quality or power that we "own" and exercise individually, and that *everything*, including our precious self, is nothing but consciousness?

Now, stand up with the book in your hand. Going only by what you see, here and now, not what you think or believe or remember ...

Look at your feet.

Now move your gaze up your body.

Look at your ankles,

Your knees,

Your hips,

Stomach,

Chest,

Can you see any further up your body?

Going by sight alone, not what you believe or feel, can you accurately describe what you *see* where your head is supposed to be?

We were taught that we are our body and that somehow, by some mysterious, unknown process consciousness has appeared *in it*. We have assumed this for so long that we don't even question it. Isn't it time we looked to see for ourselves? Does consciousness appear in our body or is it *our body that appears in consciousness*?

See for yourself right now. Put down this book, look down at your body and ask yourself, "Is consciousness appearing in my body or is it my body that is appearing in this consciousness?" Don't go by your learned assumptions; just look openly and honestly, as if for the first time.

Then ask, "Could this body even appear without consciousness? Could *anything* appear without this consciousness here?"

What are we then? Are we our body as we have been told or are we consciousness, as we can *directly observe* for ourselves? So, what then *is* our body? Could it be consciousness also?

## A Disillusioning Experience

*"Don't take yourself too seriously, because there isn't one."*
—Wei Wu Wei

When we see a magician do a trick we are fooled by an illusion. But when we see how the trick is done the illusion falls away by itself. It dissolves, the illusion is removed. We have been dis-illusioned.

That is what this book is all about. Awakening to reality is simply recognizing what-we-are. This has been called a great esoteric secret. But it is an open secret because no one is hiding it and we don't need to find it. Most wouldn't understand or believe it even if it were told to them, yet it is already given to everyone. It is simply a matter of getting rid of the illusions that are obscuring what *already is*. This great esoteric secret is a secret only because it is hidden by our own illusions. And as with all illusions, the trick is a matter of misdirection. While we are intently watching one thing, the real deception is accomplished somewhere else.

What we think we are is an illusion. This illusion is misdirecting our attention so we cannot see what is really happening and what we really are. We are so busy taking care of the imaginary self-image we don't look back (inward) and notice what-we-are and that the self is just a concept and is not real. So, it is not a matter of *adding* anything new but of *losing* our illusions in the form of concepts and learned assumptions. We think we have only ourselves, so we cling tightly to this false foundation. Yet it is not real and if we could just see through it, we could have the whole universe.

As has already been said earlier, there are two basic illusions at the root of all our mental suffering, indeed, of all the world's suffering. They may be hard to see, at least at first. But, before you reject this liberating insight as ridiculous or scary, let me remind you again that this insight does not require you to try to change in any way. True liberation requires no effort and no willpower, no special principles you have to remember to apply. It causes no guilt and requires no faith. It requires nothing but watching – simply your attention. That is precisely why nothing else has really worked for you. Everything happens by itself!

## The Two Illusions Obscuring Your Liberation

1. The illusion of individuality.

And, from the illusion of individuality arises;

2. The illusion of volition.

Your True Being is "all" of the One Pure Universal Consciousness which is directly known right here, right now. Investigate either illusion and it will ultimately lead you to the other. Therein lies the way to liberation and rest. Why include rest? You rest from effort. Because the sense of effort comes from the illusion of volition. For instance, when you have to *do* something it may feel hard or difficult to do. When this sense of effort disappears, you rest.

## *How Could They Be Illusions When They Seem So Real?*

Individuality and volition seem to be unarguable, but you may discover a great secret if you temporarily drop your learned assumptions and open-mindedly examine what actually is here and now. These illusions are caused by the way thought works. The thought process works by comparing and discriminating among the spontaneous living flow of percepts in consciousness, and by making symbols to represent similar groups of perceptions.

We call these symbols "names," "things" and "concepts." A name then comes to mean an object, a "thing-in-itself." Take, for instance, the idea of a tree. The flow of percepts within consciousness which we call a tree was an actual here-and-now experience, but the concept, the thought, the label "tree" is just a symbol, not the actual, present, living flow of percepts. It is a dead label, a vague mental image in memory.

What we conceive as "the world" is not really many separate things-in-themselves, but actually the present living flow of percepts in consciousness. From the moment we are born we hear the sounds that people use to represent what they are perceiving, the sound-symbols we call words. We have come to confuse these words with the actuality. At about eighteen months into our life we begin to get the "hang" of making these sound-symbols ourselves. And we soon get around to making a mental symbol for what is happening "here," where we perceive everything. This is how the body-mind point-of-view becomes a "me." Psychologists believe that this is a good thing, that we need a self-concept. That would be okay if we didn't take it too far and identify with it as what we are, if we didn't accept that pitiful, limited, shifting, helpless, imaginary self-concept for our entire being. (But then, of course, psychologists would be out of a job.)

The trouble is, we don't do this all by ourselves. We are constantly told in various ways that we are a "me," an individual, a separate thing-in-itself. The world model we learn supports this belief.

This leads to the illusion that there really is an objective "me" which is acting and being acted upon. This is the illusion of volition, and from this comes a new kind of pain. In the beginning there was only physical pain, which is helpful and even necessary to keep the body safe and working. That is a natural pain.[5] But now arises psychological pain, mental pain, to keep the conceptual "me" safe. This is an unnatural pain caused by the illusion of a "me" and the illusion that this "me" has volition. This is the illusion of "me" as an individual,

---

5. Even natural pain would not be as "painful" if we didn't identify with the body as what-we-are.

objective, actor and doer. However, this "me" is only a concept, a name, a thought. A thought can't think or act, so how could it have volition?

But this illusion, this perceptual mistake, does affect the thought process simply by being a basic concept in the belief system and world-view. Because the "volitional me" is such a basic concept it causes the development of a host of mental conditioned reflexes and actions required to save, protect and fulfill that "me."

### Why "Spirituality" Hasn't Liberated Us

All the systems of self-improvement we will find, whether philosophical or religious, assume we must add to, fix up, save and improve this individual, volitional self. You've tried them and they don't work or you wouldn't be reading this book. This is because you were trying to *fix the conceptual* self which only exists in imagination and can no more do anything than your shadow can. This is like trying to "put new wine into old wine skins." These kinds of teachings can only make things worse in the long run because they affirm the pseudo-self *which is the problem to begin with.*

These self-improvement schemes unhesitatingly accept this concept of a "volitional me" as real and put the burden of volition on the "me" to use their rules and principles to live right and to be successful. That is why they don't liberate us. Because the "me" is itself only a thought it can't think, let alone make decisions or act, either rightly or wrongly. This leads to feelings of helplessness, guilt and condemnation, because thoughts and actions simply follow the strongest urges or are inhibited by the strongest fears. But since the strongest needs have grown around securing, protecting and fulfilling the "me," that's what we do instead of following our altruistic, spiritual concepts. No wonder "living right" was so hard, so impossible. We may know what we should do, but the power to do it is another matter. We'll discover more concerning this mystery in a later chapter.

### *Is There An Easy Way To Not Be Taken In By "Self-Improvement" Teachings?*

The term "self-improvement" says it all. Any system, religious or philosophical that assumes that we are improving, motivating, freeing or saving our individual self, instead of simply seeing it as an illusion, is bound to make things worse instead of better. In short, *beware of anything that assumes an individual self and volition* – a self that needs to be fixed up or improved or "saved." There is nothing to improve or to save. That pseudo-self is the life you must lose in order to find your true life.

We may enjoy the emotion and the positive feelings and the personal acceptance by the group to begin with, but the ultimate effect of following these systems will be to actually increase our bondage and leave us feeling more self-absorbed and even more helpless.

Awakening is more often than not blocked by pseudo-self, volition-based spiritual teachings which constantly point us in the wrong direction. It doesn't seem to take much to misdirect us, whether this is just because of the way the thought mechanism works or whether there are other, more malicious forces at work.

## *Pay No Attention To The Man Behind The Curtain*

In *The Wizard of Oz*, the wizard tried to preserve his illusion by misdirection. He didn't want Dorothy and the others to see that he was really just an ordinary man controlling the illusion of his "omnipotence" from behind a curtain. In a similar way, the thought processes also protect the illusion of the pseudo-self behind a curtain – a veil of empty labels, misdirection, confusion and fear. In order to break free, we must actually see these things for ourselves, experientially, deeply. When it comes to discovering what-we-are, we can't simply accept this proposition intellectually. That doesn't work. We are then just adding more useless concepts to our store of knowledge, and not actually dis-illusioning ourselves.

All we have to "do" is to watch. We must actually watch the thought process, so we can see for ourselves how the illusion is being created. We must see how it works spontaneously, effortlessly and automatically, and see that what we *think* we are is just an idea, and nothing else.

Then, we must watch and see how decisions and actions actually happen by themselves, see how the intention to do something comes automatically, and not from a "me." It may be part of a mental conversation, a deliberation with ourselves, but notice that the conversation springs from the mind unbidden. It is not your self talking with yourself. Is there one self talking to another one? That would mean yet another self to fix up. If you quietly and carefully watch thoughts at the point of their arising you may be able to see how they often appear quietly at first, like a suggestion. Then they will be repeated again louder as they are "accepted."

Only by watching and seeing this in your own mind will it have an effect. Liberation and rest will then quietly come by themselves, not by the effort of trying to change. Actually, they were always here. There may be some confusion at first in understanding these things. But that also is the mind's illusion. It is our mindset, our world-view trying to ignore, resist and suppress these contrary facts. One may feel emotions of fear or confusion, but just keep calmly observing the mind and understanding will eventually break through and it will become obvious. What-we-are is spontaneous and effortless. Understanding is effortless. Change is effortless. As we see these things for ourselves illusions will fall away by themselves.

You see, these are not your problems, but the mind's problems. And the mind is not you or your doing. Whether they go away or not is not really your concern. It cannot be your concern. What-you-are has no concerns. Any concern felt is the mind's (the thought mechanism). In fact, if you are using these insights as "principles to apply" with one eye on the problem, it won't go away. This only identifies with it and gives it the power of belief. But you are not the mind, which is only the automatic process of thinking. You are what is perceiving the mind. You are what *knows* what the mind is thinking. You were never involved. All you have *ever done* is watch. Preposterous? No. It's laughably obvious when the illusion is discovered.

We must see that this is something that goes deeper than superficial intellectual agreement. We can't just say: "Okay, I believe it," then look for everything to change overnight. Admittedly, big things can and do happen in the beginning. But that is mostly from the thrill and relief of having finally come upon something that has the ring of truth to it, that feels promising and right. The emotion will eventually wear off and, at some point you will have to look deeper and longer at the here-and-now. We are going against long-held, strong and habitual assumptions; they won't give up without a fight. And remember, they "fight" with misdirection and illusion. This New Reality must be personally witnessed, personally explored and observed deeply and thoroughly in your own experience to manifest in actuality.

## This Understanding Is Not For Those Who Want To Be Superior

Many want a teacher to conform to their preconceived notions. This is because they want to have someone to emulate, to imitate and aspire to. This is not ordinarily considered a bad thing, but in this case it is a hindrance. We should be seeking inner understanding, not outer affectations. It is better for us to be attracted by the ring of truth rather than a charismatic, commanding or intimidating personality.

Awakening is nothing like our conceptions of what it will be like or what we expect it to be like or what we think an awakened person should be like. This is another great obstruction to insight. If we want to be thought of as a guru or master, then we are on the wrong track. Those who foster such desires, even unconsciously, are only using the teacher to maintain their own delusions.

The point here is not outer change, the way we act and appear to others, but inner change, the way the mind works. The outer follows the inner. Never try to change the "outer." Concentrate on understanding the mind through attention. This shouldn't result in becoming self-absorbed because, remember, the mind isn't you or yours. Outward change may be negligible or it may be sweeping. That doesn't really matter now. If we do this just for that reason we will miss the point altogether. It is *not you* who changes. What-you-are is, and always will be, just fine, eternal and unchanging. It is only illusion that is obscuring this, and the only thing that will change is the way the mind works. That will happen spontaneously when illusions are discovered.

This change will happen only if we are drawn to liberation and rest, drawn to want to see and understand the truth no matter what the cost. At first we may be drawn merely by curiosity or novelty or even rebellion against our own hypocrisy. But if we manage to avoid the path of least resistance by becoming distracted by something else "more exciting" or "more popular" or more what one *wants to believe,* we may realize that we are captivated by the feeling that we may just be on to something wondrous.

There may also come a time when we are at a place where we feel we just can't understand some important aspect and we just want to forget it all and get on with other things because it's driving us crazy. But we may find we can't. We can't go forward and we can't go back. It will probably happen sometime. This may be what the ancient masters called being "caught in the jaws of the tiger." But, if we just keep observing we will eventually gain the insight, often quite unexpectedly when we aren't even thinking about it. The whole secret is patient attention.

These insights often come silently, almost secretly, and one day we will realize: "Hey, I know that. That's obvious. I always knew that." And another illusion has fallen away. The illusion had us fooled.

That's because this "new" reality is not new. It is not this author's invention. We have always been what-we-are. What else could we be? It is just new to many because it has been hidden by the layers of illusion, by concepts of self and the world, and by concepts of volition and spirituality. While this illusion is very powerful and runs very deep, remember it is just illusion – not truth, not reality.

There is nothing at all mysterious or mystical in this recognition. We have missed the obvious simply because we have been looking in the wrong direction. We have been taking other people's word for what-we-are. We have been looking at the body-mind concepts as what-we-are instead of noticing where we are looking *from*. We don't see anything when we look at our source, where we are looking from, but that "not anything" is the un-noticed miracle in which everything appears. As "itself," it is pure, still, open, clarity; it is spontaneous, living. It is illumination, pure awareness. It is a higher dimension upstream of the dimension of conceptual mentation.

That is why we have such a hard time recognizing our True Being. There is nothing to see *here* where we are looking *from*. So we miss the obvious. We have been looking for a thought or concept of *something*, but not *no-thing*, not pure, clear awareness. But awareness is real while concepts are not. We have automatically accepted what others have told us instead of looking and seeing for ourselves what has always been right here, right now.

Most people usually look for what they *want* to believe – what they want reality to be instead of letting reality reveal itself as it is. They look for a religion or philosophy that reflects what they want to be true instead of what actually is. Often it is what appeals to the ego, the pseudo-self so they can feel they are one of the spiritual elite. Those who follow their religious rules such as "don't do this" and "don't eat that" and then secretly congratulate themselves on their spirituality are as far from awakening as anyone else.

We think we want the truth, but then we look for it only where we want it to be. This is like the old story about the man crawling around on his hands and knees under a street light. Someone comes by and asks him what he is doing.

"I'm looking for the twenty dollar bill I dropped," he replies.

"You lost it here?" the passerby asks, looking around.

"No," the man says, "I lost it down there somewhere," pointing down the darkened street.

"Then why on earth are you looking for it here?"

"Because the light is much better here," he replies.

We can also confuse spiritual feelings with spirituality, mystical feelings with mysticism, and holy feelings with holiness. Nor is simply acting spiritual being spiritual, acting mystical being mystical, or acting holy being holy.

What-we-are is immediately available as well as eternally safe and secure and can never be negatively affected. What-we-are suffers no pain or sorrow. What-we-are knows only love, total completion and fulfillment. Finding and knowing, experientially, what-we-are is the most significant pursuit we can ever fulfill. It is the supreme adventure.

### Enter Into Rest

After all our watching and attention, and after being dis-illusioned, what will we do? All we have to do – indeed all we can do – is to let our life be lived by what-we-are, as Terence Gray kindly tells us. This is how we can live fully, freely and joyfully, savoring every shining moment as a miracle itself.

*"This rest that you wait for has already come, and you have not recognized it."*

– The Gospel according to Thomas

Now, do Reality Meditation #5 once again.

# AM I MY BODY?

## *Reality Meditation # 6*

## The Dream Experiment

Sit or lie down quietly. Tune in on the sights, sounds, scents and sensations about you. Now try to recall a recent dream you have had.

First, notice how the dream was pure perceiving. There was no actual physical scene, only spontaneously arising perceptions. Recognize that the dreamed you and dreamed scene were interpreted from that pure perceiving. Then try to see that your present scene and self are manifested in the same manner.

Try to in-see intuitively that everything (including thoughts and emotions) is projected from and by *here* – where you think your head is. Of course real life, the primary dream, is more consistent and has greater continuity than secondary dreams, but it is still manifested in the same manner. This will be difficult to recognize at first because you will be going against the assumptions and conditioned thought patterns of a lifetime. They may be far stronger and more misleading than you suspect, so watch out. Your earlier "reality research" will have helped prepare you for this. Your conditioned thought patterns will automatically conclude something like this: "No, this is silly. It couldn't be this way. Dreams are, well, dream-like and this world is very real."

Actually, most people have had these thoughts while in a dream and have been convinced that they were awake. If this has ever happened to you then you know that maybe this isn't so silly after all. This is where the *Hand* experiment and the later *Cup and Light* experiment will help greatly to focus upon the pure, empty, still Source *here* as well as the scene "out there."

The things you have been studying are not original or new, but have repeatedly been pointed out by many masters, mystics and sages throughout history. Once the false assumptions and conditioned thought patterns are broken through it is recognized that this is obviously the way it is. Then there will be a much greater respect and admiration for the Source *here* and the awesome wonders it performs.

You will come to realize that this is the only possible answer to the great mysteries of creation and being. Do you see how God has been "with you" all the time? "For in Him we live, and move, and have our being." (St Paul, Acts 17:28) Now you can understand what that really means. This is so much more intimate and personal than imagining an all-powerful God looking down on you from the sky. You have been in Him and He has been in you and all the world is *in* this same consciousness. He, you, and the world have actually been one: the division has only been in thought, in the concepts of objective things. See how the split-mind world dissolves.

1. Ask yourself this: Without the Source *here* could or would either a "me" or this scene appear?

2. While doing this experiment always try to see and recognize that all is the pure, real perceiv-ing and not a perceiver and perceived.

3. See that all things and people are a manifestation of what you also are and neither you nor they have any independent nature of its own.

4. See how all appears effortlessly, spontaneously, without thought, from, in, and by *here*.

5. Notice the *whole*-ness, the *is*-ness, the *such*-ness, the *one*-ness.

6. Things happen, both in real life and in dreams, unexpectedly and unwelcomed (by the supposed self), but now the world becomes non-threatening because the feeling of otherness dissolves and everything is recognized to be projected from and by *here*. As "other" dissolves so does "self."

7. Try to recognize some of the implications of this awareness. See how it relates to such feelings and ideas as loneliness, fear, pain, anger, struggles, friendship, love, pleasure, joy, rest.

## For Now And Always

From now on, work with this understanding until it grows from a small glimmer once in a while to an awareness that fills all your day, every day, and even your secondary dreams at night. It will be difficult at first because of your habitual assumptions and conditioned thought patterns. Expect this and don't give up. Whenever this insight is remembered, hold it as long as you can. It will grow if you keep at it. The understanding may even be unexciting at first. It is for some. This is only because the incredible implications are not yet recognized. But it is the doorway to a world without parallel or description.

Be reminded continually that: *All* is the projection of the Eternal Light *here* where no-thing is. This is the peace that passes understanding.

## Am I My Body?

"I... touch the sky with my finger."

—William Blake

Alexander Gilchrist's *Life of William Blake*

The body seems to be the apparent source of all our suffering, but it is not unimportant or bad. It is quite miraculous and should be kept in as good condition as possible. It is also a source of enjoyment, but not to be identified with as what *you* are. It also seems that consciousness is a product of the brain, but it is not something in the body that the brain creates. It is just the opposite. It is the brain and the body that appear in consciousness, rather than consciousness appearing in a brain. The body is consciousness' way of expressing phenomenality. If you wish, you can visualize the body and brain as the way consciousness manifests the world. In order for anything to appear, there must be a viewpoint, a place in space from which to observe and interact with what is appearing. The body is this viewpoint; but it is not you.

The body is temporary; it has come and it will go. Everything that appears comes and goes. What were you before the body appeared? What will you be when it goes? Consciousness does not come and go because it is not in time. Time is in consciousness. Space is in consciousness.

It is not you who is thinking. Thoughts are not yours. You are the perceiv-ing of the thoughts just like you are the perceiv-ing of the breathing and of the heart beating. Consciousness is what knows that the thinking and breathing is happening and is what knows "I am" here and now.

We can learn a lot about the body and what-we-are by studying our dreams. Not by interpreting them, but by *studying the mechanism of dream projection* and comparing our findings with what we call "real life."

In dreams, raw sensory perceptions, sponta-neously appearing in consciousness, are instantly interpreted automatically by the conditioned psycho-somatic apparatus, which is itself a projection of consciousness. This process, using our learned world-model and the concept of space-time as the basic mechanism of manifestation, interprets these perceptions as the temporal, three-dimensional material world we have called reality. The sensory perceptions are what we call the five senses of seeing, hearing, tasting, smelling, and touching.

During our dream, as in real life, we seem to live in a world of separate, self-existing physical objects, or things-in-themselves. The people we meet in our dream are separate individuals acting by their own volition, doing unexpected and sometimes unwanted things. In the dream we seem to be living our own life, making our own decisions and acting volitionally. And others are also living their own lives and acting volitionally.

As in real life, we have limited control in the dream world. It consists of "self" and "other." We are "self" and everything else is "other," apart and separate from self, going its own way.

If we are lucky we have, at some time, had a lucid dream in which we recognize that it *is* a dream, while we are still dreaming. If we can keep from waking up and ending the dream, we can stay in it and recognize that *the whole dream is us*. Then we can do anything we want – no limitations. We can fly, we can instantly be anywhere we want, with anybody we want. We will find that both ourselves and the apparent world "out there" as well as all the apparent independently-acting other people were actually all made of the same "stuff:" consciousness. Neither we, ourselves nor anything else was actually a separate, self-existing volitional individual or thing. Our dream perceptions were just interpreted that way because that is our world-model. This happened automatically and instantaneously without our intention or knowing.

We can see that the dreamed body is the sensory viewpoint from where the dream is perceived. But are you really that body? Are you even in that body? Is it also being dreamed? Did your dream world take up any space in your bedroom? We always have all the space we need in a dream. Where does it come from? Where does it go when we awaken?

If the perceptions that become our dreams are automatically, unintentionally interpreted as a three-dimensional temporal world "out there" could it also be so with real life, the waking dream? The highest and best of the Great Masters have repeatedly told us that this is the case.

In our dream, we think we are living our life, making our own choices and deciding our own actions. And everyone else in the dream is also. Yet we find we have done odd things that seemed appropriate in our dreams that we think we would never do in reality. But haven't we also occasionally done odd, uncharacteristic things in real life too, even when we thought we knew what we were doing? Later, we realize that it was almost as if we were sleep-walking, just automatically reacting and not fully aware of our actions.

When we wake up from a dream, we realize that we weren't really living our own life in the dream. Even our own self and its actions were "being lived" or directed by something other than the dreamed "me." That "something other" was also guiding everyone and everything else in the dream. It was all created of the same substance, both self and other. It was just spontaneous perceptions automatically interpreted as self and other. And we weren't really who or what we were dreamed to be.

*"Let your life be lived by what-you-are."*
                                            —Wei Wu Wei

Who or what was living our dream for us? It couldn't be our assumed self, it was also in our dream wasn't it? Could this also be so with real life? Is there also "something other than me" guiding us, everyone and everything else?

As children we have probably ridden in the little cars or boats at the amusement park. They had little steering wheels on them and we really believed we were guiding them. But, actually, they were being guided by a little track that went down the middle of the lane. You will even see children fighting over who gets to steer. So, too, is our life being lived by what-we-are. This is not fatalism, because we are not this body, not this self who we think is steering. We *are actually* that "something other than me" that is "living" everything that appears, just as it is in our dream. We just haven't recognized it. We are still asleep and haven't awakened.

Douglas Harding once remarked to me: "I never know what I am going to do from one moment to the next." Of course he was just saying what should be obvious to us all. Yet to many it would sound peculiar because they think they are in volitional control. As Inspector Clouseau from the Pink Panther movies often said: "Everything I do is carefully planned in advance!"

The only thing we can know for sure about what we call our existence is that there is consciousness appearing here and now, and perceptions are appearing in this consciousness. Nothing further can ever actually be proven – not our individual self nor the world "out there." Even Descartes' famous statement, "I think, therefore I am" assumes (wrongly) that he is an objective individual who is the thinker of the thoughts. Actually all we can say is "I am."

*"When the dreamer awakens he is absolute absence."*

−Wei Wu Wei

# ISN'T THERE A "ME" SOMEWHERE?

## *Reality Meditation # 7*
## The Great Impostor

**F**ind three or four friends and ask them to do this experiment with you. You'll all have an interesting time.

Everyone stands in a circle.

1. Announce: "There is an impostor among us." Then read the next steps to the group.

2. Do you see anyone in the group who might be impersonating you?

3. What if someone looked exactly like you? Would you immediately know that person was an impostor?

4. Why?

5. So, the obvious conclusion is that anyone you can see, couldn't be you because you are who is *seeing* them. They are your objects. You (subject) are who is seeing them (object).

6. Now, close your eyes

7. Think of yourself. Say: "me."

8. Could this "me" you are seeing in thought be what you are?

9. Are you the "me" you see in thought or are you *what is seeing* the thought?

10. Should not the same hold true for thought as for sight?

11. So, the conclusion once again is, anyone you can see, even in thought, couldn't be you, because you are what is *seeing*. "Me" is your object. You (subject) are who is seeing "me" (as object).

12. Who then is the impostor?

13. Why then have you been living for this impostor, "me," all these years?

14. Can who is seeing the "me" *ever* be seen in thought? Of course not. Any self seen in thought would be your object, simply an observed thought or concept, thus not what you are as subject (what is observing).

The learned, conditioned way of thinking of our self (as an object) may lead us to assume that this is simply nit-picking, mere sophistry. On the contrary, it reveals a very fundamental flaw in logic concerning our identity, one which is responsible for all our misery. Indeed it is responsible for all the suffering in the world, and is keeping us from a new life beyond our greatest imaginings.

## A Thought Can't Think

The great Ch'an Master, Hsi Yün (Huang Po) said: "A perception cannot perceive," which also means that a thought can't think. He was referring to the fact that the thought-of-self, the objectified, conceptual "me" we perceive in thought and identify with as our self couldn't be who is thinking because it is merely a thought, a perception itself.

It may be a bit unsettling at first to realize that *any* self we think of could not be what we are, because we feel strongly that we must be able to define ourselves in some way. Let us see what happens when we do identify with this "me" which we have defined in our minds.

As we noted in the experiment, the "me" seen (and felt) in thought was our object. We have defined our self as that. However, we found we were not that, but were what was observing this self. Yet we have become identified with this observed self and regard it as us. This I-concept – "me" – then, is an *objectified* self. When we regard our self as an object, whether it be a purely mental object or a physical object such as our body, we accept all the implications and consequences of being an object.

## The Implications

Let us pause for a moment to examine the implications of identifying with this objective, illusory self, the self-concept. An objective self must necessarily be subject to space and time as are all objects.

### Why we feel alone

Spatially, "me" is separate and apart from everything else, thus the self-concept can only appear as an isolated entity separate and apart from all others.

### Why we fear death

Temporally, all material objects including objective entities are transient and temporary. The objective self therefore must come and go. We call it birth and death.

### Why we are controlled by desires and fears

All objects are subject to the laws of cause and effect and thus are affected by everything that happens. Being only an objectified image in one's mind, the self-concept is a precarious thing, affected by every thought and by every circumstance. Everything is interpreted as to whether it means good or bad for this self.

### Why we become self-centered

All thoughts are conditioned by the self-concept. All emotions, interests and actions are then relative to what bodes good or ill for the imaginary self. Our self-concept is unstable and changes moment by moment, affected by circumstances, others' perception of us, our shifting emotions, and so on.

## Volition

The self-concept gives rise to the concept of volition. Volition, we will find, is an illusion born of an illusion. As the law of cause and effect works in the thought processes, the self-concept (the first illusion) interferes with and alters the interpretation of the world. It causes everything to be interpreted relative to the self-concept. Thus, being bound by cause and effect, as all objects must be, means that an objective entity could have no free will.

## Why we have trouble with self-control

One of the effects of this grand illusion is that thoughts, emotions and actions are interpreted as initiating from and belonging to the self-concept and thus controlled by it (the second illusion). Thoughts and actions are interpreted as something "done" by the self-concept "me." However, being only a concept itself and not actually anyone at all, the self-concept has no ability to will or perform any act on its own.

Self-centered thought and action then is the inescapable effect of a cause, the self-concept.

## Isn't There A "Me" Somewhere?

*"Why are you unhappy?*
*Because 99.9 per cent of everything you think,*
*And everything you do*
*Is for yourself—*
*And there isn't one."*

–Wei Wu Wei

Because of the original illusion of the world as populated by separate, pre-existing things in themselves, we have assumed that everything that happens must be done by a someone or a something. This we call "cause and effect." Therefore, we assume thinking has to be done by a someone or a something, so we assume it is done by "me."

We have always felt "me" here, in this body. But where is it? Can we ever find this "me" other than a vague feeling or an imagination of it? Once again, we must actually look for one and find out from experience that it doesn't exist. Can you find any "me" who is doing the thinking, or only the process of thinking? (In which "me" is just one of those thoughts.) We have been identified with our thought process and with a dead concept: "me." When we can find only the concept "me," we can then begin to realize that we have been tricked out of our true identity, our true being and out of life itself.

However, what at first may seem to be the loss of everything, including ourselves, turns out to be the attainment of everything. As what-we-are, consciousness, the unmanifest Source, we are nothing; as manifest phenomenality we are everything – the entire universe.

The only thing that is obscuring this is the illusion that we are an individual self trapped in an individual body living on a huge ball of dirt whirling blindly through an infinite, unknowing, uncaring cosmos.

We are born alive and unbound
We are free and "at large"
As no one and everyone
Then we are taught we are a self
The illusion of self begets volition
Volition begets effort
Effort begets responsibility
Responsibility begets burden
Burden begets bondage
Bondage begets guilt
Guilt begets death
But it doesn't have to be this way
We can rise from the dead
Though we have to lose our life
(The one we think we are)
To find it (what-we-are)

Now, do Reality Meditation #7 once again.

# AM I MY MIND?
## *Reality Meditation # 8*
## Free As A Bird

1.  Sit quietly and simply observe your thoughts as they appear. Stay objective and do not get caught up in them and forget what you are doing. Try to notice *how* they appear, and *from where.*

2.  You will notice that they appear *before* you decide to think them. Your only "decision" may be to repeat them sub-vocally, and even that decision appears unbidden. It just seems as though you decided to think that thought because you think the thought is yours. Scientific experiments have proven that action is often initiated *before* a person is consciously aware they have even decided to act.

3.  Now compare these "internal" observations with watching a bird as it flies across the sky. Did you bid it to appear? Did you claim ownership for the bird because it appeared? No, you just noticed it and allowed it to fly on.

4.  If your thoughts appear unbidden, why do you claim ownership or control?

5. Do you try to stop the bird in flight because you don't want it there? No, because it is just part of the scenery, and by not feeling any sense of ownership you remain detached. The bird is simply one sight among many.

6. Can you see that as habitual thought patterns form around the illusory self they are triggered by association?

7. If you recognized that thoughts do not belong to the illusory self, or to any self, but were simply part of a cause and effect chain (as was the bird), wouldn't that remove the power of negative thoughts? You don't have to stop them: simply remaining detached removes their control. They are just part of the scenery.

## Am I My Mind?

*"For long years a bird in a cage,
today, flying along with the clouds."*

–Zenrin Kushu

Where does our mind fit into this new model of reality? We have been told, and we believe, that we have a mind and it is what we use for thinking. We must once again look for it ourselves. Can we really find a mind in here somewhere? We can find the idea "mind," but not any thing or object that is a mind. Is there some mysterious ghost-like field hovering around our head? What we do find, though, is simply *thinking*, which includes remembering.

Further observation shows us that a verb, an action called *the process of thinking* has been conceptualized as a noun, and thought of as a thing, an object called "the mind." But actually we have no mind: it is the process of thinking that is happening. It's like asking: "What happens to my fist when I open my hand?" or "Where does my lap go when I stand up?" "Fist" and "lap" are examples of an action being taken for a thing – a verb becoming a noun. (Although a fist in the nose still hurts just as much!)

Because of this habit of objectifying, we believe that a "something" or a "someone" must always be doing whatever is happening. For example, we say: "The wind is blowing." But, what is the wind other than the blowing? What, then, is the mind other than the thinking? We can say that the brain is thinking, and that would be right. But don't forget that the brain is an organ of the body and the body is manifested via the living dream. It is believed that consciousness appears in the brain, yet, when you go by the observed reality, it is the brain which appears in consciousness.

You are what is aware of the dream. You are the dream-ing, not the dreamer. You are what is knowing what is being dreamed and it is this knowing that makes what is appearing, real. You are what it is happening *in*. It is not happening *to* you, it is happening *in* you, via the basic concepts of space-time. They are interdependent concepts like subject-object – time is the subject aspect, and space is the object aspect. This is why it is easier to grasp what space is, but not easy to grasp what time is. Time, as the subject aspect is the observer, where you are looking *from* and therefore not observable. Time, as duration, is the unseen aspect of phenomenal manifestation. We need the three spatial extensions, height, width and depth *and* the temporal extension, duration, for the manifestation of phenomenality. The spatial aspect is what you are looking at and therefore the observed.

Whenever the word "mind" is used in this book, it refers to the *process* by which thinking automatically happens. "Who" is there to use it? Is there someone controlling it like a man driving a car or riding a stubborn mule? When we are identified with it, it seems the other way around. It drags us anywhere it wants. Instead of it serving us, we are it's unwitting slave.

By seeing that the mind is not you or yours and that its thoughts are not your thoughts, the power of identification, and thus belief, is removed from negative fearful thoughts and emotions and they can be more easily ignored. They don't have to be denied or suppressed, which just gives them power. Simply recognize that they don't belong to you and you can remain detached.

Emotions are not you or yours, but they are not bad either. In fact, even some of the "unpleasant" human emotions will still exist, (anger, sorrow, etc.) but now they are drained of negative power and a new, deeper, solid emotional level is recognized that sustains, uplifts and empowers you as needed. You can actually experience emotions more fully when they don't have control over you.

Robbed of identification, attention and belief, negative thoughts and emotions lose power and weaken. And the mind is just a source of information or conceptual knowledge. Some of it is good information, some of it is not. If there were such a thing as a "Mind Store," an information store, like a department store, you wouldn't assume that everything in it was yours and that you had to use it all. You would only "buy" what was useful and ignore the rest, even though many useless items are being promoted and advertised to make you want them and to make you think you need them.

It is fear and concern for the imaginary self that keeps us involved with the mind. That is also what keeps it stirred up and active. It may sound unbelievable now, but you really don't need it to live your life properly. Your True Being always knows what to do and will spontaneously act appropriately according to the needs of the moment, silently and without mentation or deliberation. To truly "lose one's mind" is a good thing: it happens when you see that you have never had one.

You don't have the "problem" (whatever it may be) or any fear. You never did. There is no-one to have it. It is the mind's problem because of the way it manufactures concepts. The mind has invented a concept of itself as "me," and somehow is able to pull off the charade that this pseudo-self has volitional control over it. What a grand put-on! And it works as long as we don't examine it too closely and try to pin it down. This false self "me" which is planted in the thought process keeps us from doing this by keeping the pot stirred up with fear and confusion whenever we start poking around too much. But if we simply realize that the "me" we perceive *couldn't,* at the same time, be what is perceiving, we are neatly off that merry-go-round.

We are not the mind. The mind is not "ours." It goes it's own way, automatically, but will grow more quiet and relaxed as this new reality dawns.

Now, do Reality Meditation #8 once again.

# THE ORIGIN OF ALL THINGS

*Reality Meditation # 9*

## The Cup And Light Experiment

Do this experiment in the evening or in a darkened room. Situate yourself at a table and use a flashlight with the room lights out. Cut the bottom out of a small paper bag and have it handy. Read through the assignment once and then do it. To just read it and not do it is like eating the menu instead of the meal. The intellectual understanding is not nearly as important as the experiential, intuitive insight.

1. Place an ordinary cup on the table and sit down with it in front of you.

2. Just look at the cup for a moment. Notice its shape, color, texture size, and distance from you.

3. You would ordinarily say that you are seeing a cup, but let's see if that is so. Turn the light out. Now, can you see the cup?

4. Without the light, could a cup appear?

5. What has actually been removed, the cup or the light?

6. If only the light has been removed and the cup does not appear, what were you really seeing? A cup, or light appearing as a cup?

7. Next, turn the light back on. What do you notice? A cup and a table or light appearing as a cup and a table? Even though you know intellectually that you are only seeing light waves appearing as a cup, your conditioned way of thinking still probably insists on labeling this "one" light as different things, a cup, a table, etc. This is because the mind is conditioned to habitually focus on the *forms* and not the *light*.

8. Next we are going to notice another kind of light: the "Light" of Consciousness in which there is awareness of even the physical light and the forms that it takes. Using the paper bag, open at each end, look through it at the cup. Notice the cup that appears at the other end.[6]

9. Notice the absence of any kind of appearance here at the end of the bag nearest you. This is pure awareness or the "Light of Consciousness." Without the "Light" at the near end of the bag could

---

6. I am indebted to Douglas Harding's famous "Paper Bag Experiment" from his book *The Science of the 1st Person,* where a somewhat different experiment is performed using a paper bag.

a cup appear at the other end? Compare this experiment with steps 6 and 7.

10. *What are you really seeing?* A physical cup, phenomenal light or "Light" (Consciousness) appearing as a cup?

> *"The essential metaphysical principle is that everything cognizable is whatever we ourselves are and never anything that has any independent nature of its own."*
>
> –Wei Wu Wei

## The Origin Of All Things

"Since the beginning not a thing is."

–Hsi Yün (Huang Po)

Ninth Century Ch'an Master

"An elementary particle is not an independently existing, unanalyzable entity.
It is, in essence, a set of relationships that reach outward to other things."

–H. P. Stapp

20th Century physicist

"Things derive their being and nature by mutual dependence and are nothing in
themselves."

–Nargarjuna

Second Century Ch'an Master

"Matter is derived from consciousness, not consciousness from matter."

–Sir James Jeans

Noted British Scientist

"... things which are seen were not made of things which do appear"

–The Holy Bible

Hebrews 11:3

## Where Did Everything Come From?

**B**ecause of our conditioned model of the world, the original sensory perceptions of seeing, hearing, tasting, touching and smelling are conceptualized by split-mind and interpreted (objectified) as seer and seen, hearer and heard, taster and tasted, toucher and touched, smeller and smelled. Thus, the world appears as many separate pre-existing things, and we ourselves seem to be an individual, objective[7] entity.

This is where all of our problems and suffering originate. Only an objective entity can suffer. An objective entity is bound by the chain of causation as all objects must be. Only an objective entity can suffer gain and loss. It might even be said an objective entity *must* suffer gain and loss given that it takes on the insupportable notion and burden of volition.

Our assumption of volition is in blatant contradiction to our assumption of being an objective entity which is, by definition, bound by cause and effect. We can't have it both ways, but we don't seem to notice this huge contradiction. Choosing happens, but there is no chooser.

Our only direct, subjectively verifiable experience is the sense of "I am," which we call consciousness, and the perceiving process that happens within consciousness. The ideas of an inner (mental) and outer (physical) world are mutually-exclusive, interdependent concepts, a feature of our learned world model.

---

7. A physical, material thing-in-itself - an object.

How could the two concepts "inner" and "outer" be both mutually exclusive and interdependent? For "inner" to have meaning it must have an "outer" to compare it with and give it meaning. Therefore, its meaning excludes "outer" but at the same time "inner" is dependent on "outer" to give it conceptual meaning as its opposite. And the same is true for the concept "outer." The Principle of the comparison of opposites runs throughout the conceptualized, phenomenal world. It is at the heart of the act of conceptualizing and is actually the deeper meaning of the eastern yin-yang symbol. It is what ultimately "creates" the illusion of a world composed of many separate things-in-themselves instead of the one flow of raw percepts in Awareness. To deeply apperceive this intuitively is a big breakthrough. Continue to ponder this if it is not yet clear. Its meaning and therefore its effect runs deeper than just the intellectual level.

The basic thinking process works by comparing perceptions and interpreting them via concepts which are artificial mental symbols generalized from previous, similar patterns of sensory perceptions.

Take, for instance, a chair. There are millions of different kinds of chairs in all shapes, sizes and colors. Yet we generally know a chair when we see one. This is because certain perceptions that make up the sensory experience of a chair have commonalities such as general shape, size and functionality.

Picture these perceptions being stored in memory under a label "chair." Whenever similar perceptions are encountered, the label (concept) "chair" is used to represent the flow of all the raw sensory percepts once they have been actually experienced (seeing, hearing, tasting, touching and smelling). When we think or speak of a chair we are using these symbol-concepts.

But a chair is *not* the object "chair" nor is it the concept "chair" nor is it the word "chair" nor is it the sound "chair." It is the *present* active perceiving of the subjective sensory experience, whether it is sitting in it or falling out of it or just noticing it. There is no actual thing "chair." Chair is only the concept, the word, the symbol which may *represent* the particular perception. The actuality is the here-and-now, perceptual experience.

The symbol-concept is a convenience, but it comes with a price. By "freezing" the active perceiving into representational symbol-concepts we have come to mistake the dead symbol for the living actuality. We have interpreted the active, living flow of the present perceiv-ing into an empty, dead, symbol-concept. In other words, a thing.

You may describe a cup of hot coffee, even measure the temperature of it, but you have to personally experience "hot" to know what hot is. "Hot" is not a thing, but a subjective sensation *known only in consciousness*. Thus, hot is not hot, therefore we call it hot. Or, put another way, hot (the concept) is not hot (the actual subjective experience), therefore we call it (to communicate it) "hot" (the word which represents the concept which represents the actual sensory experience). So simple, yet so difficult to communicate.

These symbol-concepts are a way to store and represent the actual experience of groups of different kinds of subjective percepts. Thus, we can communicate these experiences to others. By using these symbol-concepts, perceptions can be more easily compared with past experiences. But by doing so, we have already taken one step away from reality. Once again, we have taken the menu for the meal.

Second-generation concepts are then generated by creating opposites from first-generation concepts. These are concepts such as hot and cold, up and down, far and near, love and hate, something and nothing, self and other. As we have just seen, opposites get their meaning by comparison with each other. They are mutually dependent upon each other, yet they get their meaning by excluding the other. It's kind of like author Lewis Carroll's mythical island whose inhabitants earned a precarious living by taking in each others' washing. *(Alice's Adventures in Wonderland)*

But now we are two steps away from reality.

We are a "self" and the rest of the world is "other." We have fallen into the illusion of a world of separate pre-existing things-in-themselves. You may think of it as falling into a lower dimension of being – a ghostlike dimension consisting entirely of ideas existing only in imagination.

Isn't it ironic that what we think is the solid, physical reality is actually imaginary and what is unseen and unknown and unfelt is the solid reality? Yet, later we will see absolute documented experimental proof that quantum physics backs this up.

The worst part is that we have also *identified* ourselves as an individual pseudo-self, a thing, a separate objective entity moving through objective time and space. We become, in effect, a tiny, impermanent, fragile, separate thing, alone and helpless in an unimaginably vast, impersonal, pre-existing universe of other things.

As a thing, we now take on the illusion of volition because the thought process, restructured around the concept of self, now assumes that "I," using "my mind," is what is deciding and acting. The feeling and sense of being the "decider" and actor appears and grows because of the concept of self as the body-mind.

## How The Carefree Living We Knew As A Child Became The Burden Of Great Effort

The concept of self as an individual body-mind and actor is what changes the way the formerly free, effortless and spontaneous thought processes work. The thought processes must now add many extra "loops" or deliberations to the original process because the effect upon the conceptual self (good or evil), of everything that happens, must now be considered. Thus is born "the knowledge of good and evil." For the interdependent concepts "good" and "evil" can only have meaning in relation to individual selves and other "things."

These extra thought loops proliferate as desires and fear begins to accumulate around the self-concept. Contradictions and frustrations also begin to accumulate because the conceptual self's "self-image" often conflicts with its actual secret desires and needs.

Not only does the body naturally need to be protected against physical harm, but now the concept (illusion) of self must also be protected. Moment by moment it calculates itself as gaining or losing according to circumstances, others' perceptions of it and its "own" actions.

The once free, effortless and spontaneous action we knew as a child is now all but paralyzed by layer upon layer of considerations involving the ever-vulnerable symbol-concept of self, mistakenly believed to be the real "I." Living has thus taken on the burden of a great effort.

This is the root of all inorganic mental illness, all conflict, crime and violence.

Now, do Reality Meditation #9 once again.

# WHO IS THE
# REAL "I"?

## *Reality Meditation # 10*
## The Self Chart

First do the "Now" and "Hand" meditations from previous chapters, then compare the columns below labeled "Self-concept" and "What-you-are."

Can you think of some more comparisons?

If you can think of some, write them below these to remind yourself later.

| SELF-CONCEPT: | WHAT-YOU-ARE: |
| --- | --- |
| (Can a thought think?) | |
| Labels for self | No labels possible |
| Appearing | Non-appearing |
| Changing | Non-changing |
| Thing | No thing |
| Limited | Unlimited |
| Dead | Living |
| etc. | etc. |

GOOD
EVIL
STRONG
WEAK
PRETTY
UGLY

137

What appears is created in and by what does not appear.

It is the habit of thinking of yourself as the label "self" and the body that has caused all your problems. You are not who you *think* you are, but pure, clear, living, Awareness itself.

## Who Is The Real "I"?

"I am, but there is no me."

−Wei Wu Wei

Consciousness is the real "I."

But what do we mean by the term "consciousness?" Consciousness should not be a noun, but a verb. However, conscious-*ing* is not a word. The word consciousness is often mistakenly used to mean its content, or what we are conscious *of*, not what consciousness actually is.

Here, in this book, it is used to mean the pure, bare sense of "am-ness," being or presence. Pure Awareness, if you will. Consciousness is not anything in itself, yet it is "this" in which everything appears and has its being. It is what *knows* what is appearing. It is what *knows* this moment. This is the foundation upon which the unmanifest Source, the Absolute, begins phenomenal manifestation by extending itself temporally and spatially.

Within consciousness − this tiny infinitesimal point of awareness, this bare, tacit sense of "I am" − appears the whole universe. From within consciousness, percepts spontaneously appear which are cognized ultimately as "living in the world." This is the illumination of consciousness.

Consciousness is what *knows* I know and knows what is being thought, but never thinks itself. This is what knows every experience, but is not the experiencer. This is what knows everything that appears, but never appears itself. Consciousness is "upstream" of all that appears – upstream of both "something" and "nothing," being neither. It is the ground of being in which something and nothing appear and are known.

This is what we are as "I."

Now, do Reality Meditation #10 once again.

# THE SECRET OF NON-VOLITIONAL LIVING

*Reality Meditation # 11*

## You Are Pure Consciousness

What is it that knows this moment?

What is it that is aware of your thoughts and feelings?

That's "it."

What is it that *knows* you are?

What is it that *knows* "I am?"

That's "it."

The above is just a little puzzle to confound the linear, dualistic thought process and point to the non-linear, the non-dual.

This "it" is what-we-are – nothing more. Everything that appears is just raw percepts spontaneously and magically arising in this Pure Awareness. Take away what appears in consciousness and you have the bare, tacit sense of being, of "I am." Not as anyone or anything, not a "me," just am-ness. This is what-you-are.

If you could turn off everything that appears in consciousness and just have consciousness itself, there would be no world, no body, no thoughts or feelings, no self, no "me." Just the bare sense of am-ness. This is what you are as "I."

So then, how do we re-cognize we are this pure "am-ness?"

Sit quietly and focus on this Pure Consciousness, this bare, silent sense of am-ness. Ignore all thoughts that arise. This brings the linear and non-linear "minds" or mentation processes into balance and harmony. It allows the non-linear, intuitive understanding of the unconscious to surface.

It may seem that there are multiple consciousnesses, one in every body, but this is not so. There is only one consciousness. This One Consciousness is the sense of "I am." This is the one and only sense of "I am" we *all* know as "I." There are many minds, many bodies and many worlds appearing in this One Consciousness. These minds identify with the body that appears with it in consciousness and understands or cognizes this to be an individual "me" living its own life in a world which is separate from "itself." Nothing could be further from the truth.

When this identification with the individual self dissolves, this is "liberation." Yet no "one" was really liberated. In other words, when the mental habit of identifying yourself with an individual, volitional entity is broken, the mind is freed and ceases it's frantic activity.

The concept of a self does not have to be destroyed – it is neither good nor bad in itself. It still has its uses in conversation. But the thought process itself no longer holds any power of attachment, it is not associated with what-you-are. It no longer needs to constantly calculate whether what is happening is good or bad for the self. All the feelings of effort, fear and need are no longer stirred up, and for the most part, the thought process has little left to do.

Imagine what that would be like. Clear, effortless, being, totally in and totally one with the moment. All is as it should be. This is what has been called by the ancient masters "suchness" or "such-as-it-is-ness."

It can take a long time to actually realize that *everything* that appears in any way is not you or yours such as the mind, the body, the will, emotions, knowledge, talents, possessions and so on. You will unconsciously, out of habit, accept thinking as *your* thoughts, as something *you* are doing. Can you now see it is not? You will unconsciously, out of habit accept feelings and emotions as *your* feelings and emotions. They are not. You will unconsciously, out of habit accept your knowledge as yours. It is not. You are what is aware of the thoughts, feelings, emotion, knowledge. You are what knows it is appearing "here."

In truth, it is not even you who is accepting these things as yours. There is no "you," so "it" cannot be doing anything – right or wrong. What-you-are is not doing anything either. It is just the thought process that has gotten tangled up in a strange recursive loop because of a bit of faulty programming: identification of this same process with its own invented self-concept. That's all. It has never affected any "you." It surely has nothing to do with, nor can it affect in any way, what-you-are.

What you are does not think, feel or know. "It" doesn't have to, it just *is*. "It" is neither something nor nothing, but what they both appear in. It is not even an "it" but is the is-ness of everything.

## The Secret Of Non-Volitional Living

The most important discovery you can ever make.

> "The wild geese do not intend to cast their reflection
> The water has no mind to receive their image."
>
> —Zenrin Kushu

Remember, if you can, how it used to be when you were very young. The self-concept hadn't yet fully taken over the freedom and joy of just being; you lived in the present, effortlessly and spontaneously. Each day was eagerly faced, not reluctantly, as something to be endured, but as a joyous adventure.

This New Reality we have been investigating is really that *original* reality we were born into, with no concepts such as "self" and "other." We did not localize our self as anywhere or anyone. But this was gradually forgotten as we grew up. Alas, we didn't really grow up, we grew down – down into a lower dimension of shadows and illusion instead of substance, down into the dungeon of individuality. Once in a while we half-remembered this freedom with deep nostalgia, wondering whatever happened to that specialness, that effortless joy and open wonder we once knew long ago. Where did it go? The harder we try to be happy, the more elusive it is.

Actually, the good news is, it is *still here*. This effortless living never went anywhere. It is still here and has always been here. It has instead become veiled and distorted by illusion, an illusion that arises because of the way the thought mechanism works and because we have accepted what others have told us we were. They all live in their own version of the same illusion, and have unwittingly passed the deceptive virus of an objective self on to us.

## What Non-Volitional Living Is Not

It has been stated in earlier chapters that this is not a doctrine, philosophy or religion. It is not a set of rules that tell us how to act or methods that we must apply to our behavior. Instead non-volitional living activates *automatically* as understanding (reality) dawns.

However, a few misunderstandings need to be addressed up front to help us stay on the right track.

*Non-volitional living is not about self-surrender.* There is no self to surrender and no one to surrender it. That would take two selves, one to be surrendered and the one who "has it" to surrender.

*It is not self-renunciation or self-denial.* You don't have to deny or remove the self. It is not something to be given up or cast off. What is cast off, and by whom? You don't have to deny what is not you or yours.

*Non-volitional living is not self-effacement.* The self is not something that must be torn down, stamped out and replaced with a better one, because it never truly existed.

*And it is not a model for concocting some kind of political or religious utopia.* It cannot be legislated through laws or government. This is not something that can be accomplished through any form of state-run collective. Such "social engineering" efforts are absurd and have repeatedly been proven a failure in the past. They are doomed from the outset, given the nature of the illusory, objectified self. Individuality is not, and cannot be merged into some great collective or group ego. What-we-are is non-dual and that is neither someone nor no-one, but is "upstream" of both conceptual opposites.

And please don't try to imagine that you are a *part* of a conceptual God or some great Consciousness somewhere. There are no parts and no-thing to be a part of. The non-dual is not even really one, as that would then infer that "it" was something objective as an object, a thing or an entity. Such mystical-sounding concepts as "we are all connected" may have some meaning at some level, but without exposing the illusory self it is still just another jail cell in the same old dungeon of individuality.

Our vocabulary doesn't even need to change. Words such as "I," "me," "mine," "myself" and so on are still necessary for communicating normally. We will just interpret them differently. Trying to avoid them is needless and cumbersome. Only when we are speaking of these matters do we need to be more careful for clarity.

In short, we don't have to get rid of any self. When we have deeply and utterly re-cognized that there never was one to begin with, and could never be one, the mind's identification with it will break.

Deputy-Minister: *But I am a profane man, I hold an Office, how could I study to obtain the Way?*

Shen Hui: *Very well, Your Honour, from to-day I will allow you to work on understanding only. Without practicing, only reach understanding, then when you are deeply impregnated with your correct understanding, all the major entanglements and illusory thoughts gradually will subside....In our school we indicate at once that it is the understanding which is essential without recourse to a multitude of texts.*

— Shen Hui, h.5.

*Yes, but Shen Hui was there to promote the understanding: we only have him as one of a 'multitude of texts'.*

*Yes, he says it - understanding can suffice. But we must 'live' that understanding - noumenally of course!*

— From the beginning of "All Else Is Bondage: Non-Volitional Living" by Wei Wu Wei

## The Secret

Time and time again you have vowed in good faith to take control of your life and live it the way you know you can and the way you have decided you must. You were inspired to explore the awesome wonders and mysteries of a higher life. Many times it has looked as though you had finally found some answers and the power to succeed in your quest. Encouraged, you enthusiastically threw yourself into the new effort, the new path. Perhaps you actually seemed to succeed for a time.

But then, just when it seemed as though you had things under control, something unexpected happened and you reverted to the old way again and did exactly what you had resolved not to do. You were surprised at yourself for falling prey to an old weakness you thought you had conquered. Often the mind will try to rationalize your actions away as necessary, but if you can be honest about it you will realize what you did was wrong. Feeling defeated and discouraged you once again begin searching anew for a better way to attain the higher life.

## What Is This Mysterious Power That Makes Us Do What We Have Resolved To Not Do?

There are two parts to this secret. This is the first part:

*Every time we attempt to exercise our volition to control the needs, behavior and weaknesses we dislike in ourselves, the mind supposes that a "me" is willing it and doing it. And the moment this "me" is considered, all the needs and desires associated with it are awakened and energized.*

In short, any attempt at willpower will at the same time activate the very behavior you are trying to stop. Do you see the catch? It's the "Great Joke."

Stop here and think about this for a moment.

The secret above is virtually never shared because it is so seldom understood. Yet this is the heart of non-volitional living. This is that mysterious power that makes us do those "stupid" self-defeating things that seem okay at the time, but land us back where we started. Later we wonder: "What was I thinking?!" This secret is always lurking in the background totally unsuspected and is the reason why every method of self improvement and self-discovery you have ever tried has ultimately been disappointing or has actually made matters worse.

Here is how it happened. Early in your life the conceptual thought process formed the beginning of a concept of self by objectifying that same thought process and incorporating it with the physical body.

This mentally confined you to a psyche-soma and you visualized yourself as a mind within a body. That caused the thought process to discover a host of new needs related specifically to protecting and reinforcing this limited, imaginary objectified entity – "me" – which existed merely as insubstantial images and feelings appearing only in thought. All the while your real, concrete identity has unceasingly been the miraculous, eternal, living Consciousness in which this dead self-concept – as well as the entire universe – appears and has existence.

However, any sense of that higher, unlimited life was soon lost as the focus of the mind's attention was captivated and ensnared by the new conceptual self and its ever-multiplying needs and demands. It is those now teeming needs spawned by the formation of that pseudo-self that continue to be the focus of the thought process to this very moment.

Even if this is now comprehended, the catch is that, because of the conditioned, habitual assumption that the pseudo-self is the actor, the doer – the "me" – any attempt to deny or suppress that pseudo-self or those needs, *actually gives them more power*. This is because the thought process automatically accredits any such effort to that same pseudo-self. This just reaffirms the pseudo-self which then activates its engendered needs.

Thus any direct effort you make to get rid of this conceptual self or the unwanted behavior that has resulted from it can actually create the *opposite* effect. Such efforts of willpower only strengthen the power of the conceptual self by accepting it as something real that has volition, that can act of itself. But though it can no more act of itself than your shadow can, simply being "me" empowers, arouses and triggers, all the pseudo-self's associated needs. So, can you now see that when the pseudo-self is thus "used," it actually *activates* the very desires and actions the mind has associated with it? It ultimately compels your actions to embody those impulses instead of the higher qualities you really intended to follow. This is why it is so frustrating when we "do what we hate," instead of what we resolved to do.

You are not the first person to have this mysterious problem. The apostle Paul had the same trouble 2000 years ago. "For that which I do I understand not; for what I would, that do I not; but what I hate, that I do." (Romans 7:15) Sound familiar? He experienced this problem and also discovered the same solution we are now discovering.

*The fact that the exercise of our supposed volition activates the desires and needs associated with the conceptual "me" is the most important discovery that can be made.* It is at the very core of our dilemma and, indeed, of all the problems of civilization.

When the conceptual self is assumed to be someone real, it validates all the self-related needs, desires and fears, likes and dislikes. They have been adopted to protect and maintain this very vulnerable, severely limited imaginary self. Your present world-view has literally been built upon this mental image of a mind in a body. It now seems so self-evident that it affects everything you think and say and do.

The end result is, the harder you try to improve it or even get rid of it, the stronger and more entrenched it seems to get. It's like a dog chasing its own tail: the harder we try to change, the harder it is to change.

The more selfless we try to be, the more selfish we become, and the more we fight against a vice we have, the more we will want to do it. The more we fight a fear we have, the more we focus on it and the more frightening it becomes. The harder we try to be happy the more unhappy we get. And so it goes with anything rooted in the conceptual self.

Remember, *any* self you think of as an entity can *only* be an unreal, conceptual self.

## How To Escape This Paradox

The second part of this secret is this: *Volition is also an illusion. It is completely imaginary.*

True volition has never actually happened. Your life is completely spontaneous right now, this very moment. If the conceptual self is an illusion, then its volition, its ability to act, can only be a secondary illusion. Can a thought think or act?

Watch the mind as it operates. See if thoughts and actions really come from any self. Or do they just appear by themselves, one thought leading to another? Doesn't it simply feel like they are from "yourself" because you have always assumed they were? Where does that feeling come from? Could it be automatic too? Even when you deliberate on this very subject, where does that come from? A self? Can you find it? Who is looking for it? Or is it just assumed it must be "me" doing it?"

Watch the mind. Where do your intentions come from?

Do they come from any entity or do they just spontaneously appear?

Where do your decisions come from?

Where do your ideas come from?

Where do your fears come from?

Where do your desires come from?

Where do your likes and dislikes come from?

Where do your feelings come from?

Where do your opinions come from?

Where do your questions come from?

Where do your answers come from?

Where does your understanding come from?

Are any of them really *yours* then?

It all boils down to where your thoughts come from and where your actions come from. Is any of it really from you or your "doing?" How could it be? Can you see how the "loss" of ownership of these things is actually liberation?

It is at this point that some readers may jump to the conclusion that non-volition is the same as not-doing and not-acting. But if volition is "doing," non-volition is *not* "not-doing." Not-doing is still volition in its negative, passive aspect. It still assumes a self that is purposely not doing anything. We are "doing" not-doing. So non-volition is *neither* doing *nor* not-doing.

What does this mean? And more important, how do I do that? It sounds so complicated and impossible, but that's only because we are still asking the same futile questions: "What can I *do* about it? What should I *do* about it?"

If volition is illusory, then these are non-questions. How can you do or not do anything about it if both your doing and not-doing is an illusion? Yes, of course doing and not-doing happen, but no "you," no "me," no "self" is doing it or is the agent of it. It is completely spontaneous. Urges – automatic reactions – are working deep within the thought process and emerge as thoughts, feelings, actions. If volition is an illusion then non-volitional living means that you are *unable* to either do or not do anything. Why? Because there is no "you." You are not anyone, so there is no one to either do or to not-do. Non-volitional living is not something to do, it is just a present *fact*.

Right now you are neither doing nor not doing. You just need to realize it. That's all there is to it.

What a load off your back! You can relax. Most important, the mind can relax. You will find "yourself" still doing what is to be done, but now, it is without the sense of effort. Nothing has changed except the way you see (in-see) it.

When this identification with the pseudo-self snaps it allows the urges to propagate from an even higher source *prior to* the body-mind. Spontaneous action springs from what-you-are. This is true, original action. Before that happens it is all *re-actions, all cause and effect.*

The illusion of volition is what caused the feeling of effort when we had to do something we weren't interested in doing. Volition implies an objective agent, an entity, as the initiator and there isn't one. What-you-are is not involved in this dilemma, never has been, never will be. It has never been a problem for what-you-are.

It certainly may seem like a problem to you right now but it is simply a confusion within the thought mechanism where it has mistaken this same automatic thinking process for its actual being. Just as we mentally create a thing, an object, out of what is really just an action – such as a "fist" mistaken for the *action* of balling up our hand – the thinking process has objectified its own action of thinking into an entity, "I," as the thinker. "I" am not that process. "I" am the silent, still Consciousness in which not only that process but the rest of the universe is spontaneously appearing. This Consciousness has no appearance, no qualities itself but is the "source" from which this moment and everything in this moment derives its actuality, its "is-ness."

## The Consequences Of This Radical Understanding

Just recognizing that there is no "me," no self, totally removes "you" from the situation. You are not a participant. You have never been involved and never can be. You don't have to try to get disentangled from it.

Realizing this will help to release the mind's focus from the relentless grip of the self-concept and allow the mind to begin to refocus "upstream" or "prior to" the thought process to this Awareness, this Pure Consciousness.

When it becomes clear that you are not this pseudo-self, you will experience a release from the sense of frustration, condemnation and guilt for the actions and thoughts caused by the mind's identification with the pseudo-self. While you may still be sorry for the effect of past actions you will be released from the cycle of guilt and condemnation. This will allow the attention to refocus "upstream" of conceptual thought.

## Moral And Ethical Values

The question may arise: "Are moral and ethical values actually bad then if they cause the opposite results?" Of course not. Here is why. They can *expose* the pseudo-self and deepen the understanding of what is happening and what is real.

We have been taught since we were children that it is bad to be selfish, and that selfishness is wrong because it is believed that altruism is better and it helps society to work better. Actually, we don't really want to be unselfish. We know that we will just be taken advantage of by the other selfish people. But a better reason for unselfishness is that it can expose the powerlessness of the conceptual self and its supposed will. We can't help it, we can only hide it. When understood, selfishness is no longer something to be ashamed of, for it can be our teacher.

However, it is possible for some people to *appear* to have conquered the self by their willpower and spirituality and become "selfless." Possibly some have. But the mind can be very devious. It can learn to act and to appear quite saintly. Ironically, the "self" gratifies itself by appearing selfless. And we might even believe that we have indeed conquered our selfishness ... mostly.

But actually, if you watch the mind closely and honestly you can see that the habitual identification with the concept of self is still the fundamental assumption ruling the thought process, and it is capable of breaking forth at any time. You will discover that the mind has just learned ways to hide its worst and most obvious manifestations. The desire to appear good has become strong enough to suppress the most selfish actions.

This operation can become so unconscious that we can even fool ourselves and we might even begin to feel we actually have become a relatively good person by our own efforts. However, the mind is still a slave to the self-concept and the multitude of needs it has spawned.

If you discover this, don't be dismayed or discouraged. This is real progress. You don't have to fix it: just exposing it in this way will eventually dissolve it.

For the thought process, self preservation amounts to the same thing as preservation of the pseudo-self because that is who it thinks it is. That has become its main purpose. Observing the mind will reveal that it also tries to suppress the selfish impulses with guilt and fear of discovery. If we have enough guilt or fear over some desire or action the self can, to some extent, suppress its expression. Again, we may even believe we have conquered it. But you will discover that it always finds other ways to be expressed.

When there is no longer any identification with the conceptual self there is no one who can be guilty or condemned. Thoughts and actions will no longer be enslaved and affected by the needs created because of it. Living is once again effortless and joyous. Can you see how the sense of effort is just a feeling, a tension that grew from the presence of the self-concept and its imaginary volition?

All of the ways we may try to deal with our behavior are ultimately destructive if we don't understand what is really happening in the mind. Without this understanding, self-improvement methods actually strengthen the power of the self-concept and undermine our character, our basic humanity and drive us into living in a world of duplicity, deceit and rationalization. In order to appear the way we want, to ourselves and others, we must deal with the conflicts and dilemmas lurking beneath that facade, to keep the lid on it. Secretly, we still suffer, have little joy and little peace.

This can become so much a part of our everyday life that we come to accept it as normal. Indeed, we are even told it *is* normal. But just because it is a world-wide affliction and may be common, it is *not* normal.

This is precisely why some have set out to sincerely dedicate their lives to living virtuously but have ended up as bitter, angry, judgmental hypocrites. Most of us, though, are not trying to become saints, we just want to learn how to cope with the everyday things like dreading our job. However, if we know about the pseudo-self, the higher values can be used to expose how they affect the working of the thought process. Then we can see how the pseudo-self is the source of our dislike of having to go to work, as we associate our job with effort, effort with volition and volition with the "me."

If you are a golfer, even playing golf might lose a lot of its fun if you had to do it for a living. For the rest of us, even _____ (fill in the blank with your favorite pastime) would lose a lot of its fun if you had to do it eight hours a day for a living.

## *Focusing On Identification While The Illusory Self Dissolves*

Dealing with the identification with the pseudo-self first involves seeing that you are already free at this moment. There was never anyone to be affected. You always have been free, but weren't aware of it. None of this false self has been you or yours. And now that you have no stake in the outcome, you can celebrate your freedom. It is like living in a jail cell for a long time only to find that the door has never been locked.

Your problem was simply that "you" thought "you" were living "your" life. That's precisely why it wouldn't work. Now you can begin to consciously let your life be lived by what-you-are. It always has been, but now it can be accepted and appreciated. Without this insight you were fighting against it. Recognizing what-you-are will have an immediate effect bringing relief, joy, and a boundless sense of freedom and deep, penetrating peace. Trusting your imaginary pseudo-self to live your life is like trusting your shadow to guide you home. However, you can surely trust what-you-are to live your life. What-you-are already knows every moment of "your" life from beginning to end because it *is* every moment. It *is* your life. It will take care of itself.

So, the question is, what happens next? Do we just occupy ourselves with whatever is at hand or is there a way to deepen this experience?

Both.

You see, even though the mind, being simply an autonomic thought process, has no volitional power of its own, ideas themselves do have the power to work within it, and can divert it onto another course that can even alter the very way the mind functions. Proof of that is the way the mere presence of an idea, the self-concept, has completely enslaved it and turned it in upon itself. Ideas can trigger other thoughts and ideas through association, constructing an intricate web of cause and effect, random events, neurophysiology, stimulation and inhibition, etc., (phenomenally speaking).

Now, because you are reading this book, the ideas you are absorbing have the power in themselves to redirect the focus of attention back upstream of thoughts and concepts to notice Pure Consciousness itself. If your mindset does not suppress this insight, you will recognize (re-cognize) that this is actually what-you-are. This can reorient the mind to your Real Being and reintegrate it, allowing it to function in a new, higher way – whole, unlimited and spontaneous. It will be free to function from the orientation of the non-dual "I am" in which all appears and has its being.

The break from identification with the "self" can happen in the very first instant of looking back "upstream,"[8] and "in-seeing" the first real glimpse of what-you-are. Or it may take as long as several years after recognizing what-you-are for the full outworking. Whatever time it takes is worth it. This outworking is sometimes called "ripening." It is the outworking of enlightenment. Enlightenment is not something that happens to "you" – it is what you are. But the important thing is that from that

---

8. The Greek root word "μετανοεω" translated as "repent" is made from two words, "μετα" meaning go behind, beyond and "νοεω " meaning mind, thought, concepts, feelings.

first moment of intuitive insight, you *know* you are free.

The thought process, built upon the conceptual self, can be very devious in finding ways to preserve that identification with a "me." Your entire belief system is built upon the conviction that it *is* the "me" so this threatens the conceptual self. In fact, it may well accept much of what is in this book as the truth. It may even try to integrate this into its world-view. (After all, it does want to improve itself, to be happy and free.) But it is not even an "it." It is simply a *process*, the thinking process, not a person or a thing, definitely not you or even your doing, just an involuntary action, as a heartbeat is an involuntary action.

The mind imagines itself to be a self who has a mind. No wonder it feels burdened trying to keep this huge contradiction hidden.

The reactive thought process will still try, out of habit, to assume it is an objective, independent volitional entity. It is the habit of a lifetime, running deep in the sub-conscious. And, without actual first-hand experience, a superficial, intellectual knowledge is just not enough to fully expose the conceptual self as the illusion it is. So, focusing on Pure Consciousness and observing how the pseudo-self exists only in thought is helpful to dissolve the identification with it, and the needs that it has generated. Eventually the sense of effort will cease, and non-volitional living will operate openly and freely.

But always remember, you are already free. You have never been bound because there has never been anyone to be bound. You can always return to this profound truth: **It is only the thought process that is affected and that is not you or yours.** The feelings of fear or confusion or frustration belong to it, not to who-you-are. This is not something you have to *do*. It is something you *watch*. That is all you *can* do. And even that will happen only because you are reading it now. Reading about it plants the idea to watch the thought process. Then you will think of it and it will happen. It will change by itself.

This is why it will help to keep reading this book over and over again. Each time understanding will grow and new things will be seen. You are breaking through a lifetime of conditioned concepts and the resistance of mindset.

Even though the power of the conceptual self is pure illusion, this illusion must be fully exposed *in actual experience* for it to lose its power to affect thoughts and behavior. Just as a lie will still work if it is believed, if the mind still identifies with itself as what you are, it will still have the power to influence, delude and warp the body-mind. Until that dissolves, the effects of this understanding will not be fully realized nor fully manifested. However, that's still okay. You are removed from it. The initial discovery that you are not the self is life-changing in itself, even though it may be just the smallest glimpse. It is worth however long it takes to apperceive it fully.

Once again, nothing the mind or body does, needs, feels or has, is you or your doing. What-you-are can never suffer or be affected in any way. What-you-are has always been free. What-you-are never changes. What-you-are is pure, clear, still, eternal awareness, upstream of all that appears, of all that comes and goes, of all that is good and bad. It is *all* and yet is apart from it all. It is not an entity or "thing" or even an "it," but the shining clarity in and by which everything is appearing, which *knows* that this moment is.

## For Future Consideration

If you are adventurous you may find that you can also focus on the higher character qualities of being. Focusing on higher character qualities takes courage, even though you know that the conceptual self is still a conditioned part of the thought process, and even though you know you may be deliberately arousing the opposite tendencies. You will have "failures." You may even be accused of being a hypocrite. Indeed, the mind itself will accuse you of just that. But you will also see that there is joy in it. There is something beautiful and honorable in this endeavor above the common purpose.

Since trying to live up to higher standards only activates the needs created by the illusion of self, why shouldn't we just drop our values and do what we want?

If someone accepts that there is no such thing as volition and concludes that they can't help but act on every impulse, then that is what they will do because that is what they want to believe. They can't be helped at this point. But hopefully, they may eventually see the futility in it.

The higher character qualities stand to show us the expression of a life free from the domination of the pseudo-self. Such qualities as:

Love

Joy

Peace

Patience

Gentleness

Goodness

Faithfulness

Kindness

Self-control

And these are the basis for:

Commitment

Courage

Character

Fidelity

Honor

Truth

Trustworthiness

Sacrifice and

Personal responsibility

We are not trying to acquire these qualities, especially in order to be liberated: it is the opposite. They come from realizing you are already free. They are the manifestation of your True Being. They will appear unsought and unexpected. However, we can be manipulated and used with these ideals if we are just trying to prove to our self and to others that we have them. "Political Correctness" is a good example of how we can be manipulated this way.

The truth is, we possess the entire universe because we *are* the entire universe. It is our phenomenal manifestation.

## *You Must Love One Another*

Some spiritual leaders are fond of telling us: "You must love one another," and then congratulate themselves on being so spiritual. But we already know we should love one another. We've already tried to do it and failed. What they never tell us is *how* to do it, perhaps because they don't know themselves. We may wonder, should we just act loving or must we actually love in our heart? And even if we do manage an initial expression of love, it is hard to maintain it when it isn't appreciated or reciprocated. Now we can understand why we couldn't really love everyone unconditionally.

It is one's total belief system, our deepest unconscious beliefs and desires, that affect what choices are made and what we do. Not our volition, not our will. Volition or will does not enter into it. If doing the right thing is important enough in the belief system, whether from selfishness or fear or altruism, it will result in the action. That is why willpower sometimes seems to work, but not without encountering the previously mentioned "mysterious" phenomenon where the pseudo-self-related needs and desires are activated by the very attempt to express those qualities. However, without the aim to acquire these higher qualities, we would not have the opportunity to exercise their real value in exposing the illusory self, and discover this higher dimension.

We perceive this process of trying to choose higher principles as "making a difficult choice." We call it "deliberating" and "deciding," the tacit premise being: "Will I gain or lose?" We believe it is "me" weighing "my" options, then choosing and acting. But actually, if we really observe the process, no "me" is acting. It is simply a series of mental re-actions *and the stronger belief or urge will eventually win* and be expressed.

This "dialogue with our self" is basically an experience of rationalizing. And it all happens by itself. In fact, it is more often *after* we act that we come up with a reason why. Actions can actually begin *before* the decision to act has been made. Ask a combat pilot about this.

## *One Of The Most Common Misunderstandings Of Volition*

Bill Douglas (not his real name), a married man, had attended a seminar on these matters. Bill really took to the part about the illusion of volition, so much so that he used it as an excuse to have an affair with another woman. His reasoning was that since he had no control over his will, he just had no choice but to go along with his "real" feelings. It was inevitable, after all, he reasoned.

A few simple questions might have saved him from this mess. But at the time he probably didn't really want to ask them.

*Who had no control?* This at least reveals that the "mind" was identified with and serving the pseudo-self.

*Who wanted this woman and why?*

*Would it improve his life or could it cause more problems?*

*Would it promote happiness or just feed some immediate demands of the pseudo-self?*

*Is this the kind thing to do to his wife?*

*Would this be kind to the other woman who was also married?*

Could this at least have been an opportunity to watch how the identification with pseudo-self affects his reasoning and actions, even if he couldn't help himself? And shouldn't Bill have realized that he might not be understanding non-volition properly? Or maybe he was just looking for a good excuse to do what he wanted and not have to feel guilty about it.

Those needs he felt can never be satisfied completely because their real purpose is to sustain an illusion, the conceptual self. Feeding them doesn't make them go away. It only makes them stronger and even harder to resist the next time. Yet, often we don't care about that at the time. We may blame "circumstances" and other people and then wonder why our life is a mess, why we are still unhappy and why life is so unfair to us.

Bill's belief system used it to fulfill his more immediate and stronger urgings. And, there were consequences as it did cause him and others a lot of trouble and suffering.

### *It Is Futile To Remain Identified With The False Self While Ignoring Right And Wrong*

Bill had missed the point. The mind is very good at rationalizing a reason to do what it feels it needs to do. Though he may not have realized it, his thought process was actually trying to preserve the pseudo-self and, at the same time, avoid the constraints upon it. But as we now know, there isn't a self to keep: it's not real. Who is there to keep it and why? Its desires are not our desires. This is a way the thought process has of fooling itself into keeping the illusion of the objectified self intact and the needs it has generated and, at the same time, getting rid of those "pesky" guilt-producing moral restraints (along with simple common sense).

We can't "keep" the illusory self and ignore society's rules of conduct. Not just because it is wrong, but also because it is unworkable. The self-concept has no power in itself and identifying with it only brings more suffering and bondage.

That's why values, rules and laws originated in the first place, as an attempt to restrain the very needs that are created by the self-concept. And also, as we have now found out, those rules of conduct create a need for the illusory self to perform which *exposes* that self-illusion when we discover that it has no power of itself to act.

Only when it is exposed as not real but simply an *idea* and the identification with it dissolves, does the need for rules of conduct and laws disappear because they will then be spontaneously, effortlessly fulfilled.

However, in the meantime, before we discover that the self is an illusion, we, in our own mind, are held accountable for our actions even though we may attempt to rationalize them away. And others are caused suffering because of what we do whether we think so or not. We cannot take those parts of the path of non-volitional living we like and think we understand while (perhaps even unknowingly) leaving out the part we don't like or don't understand, and escape the consequences.

For Bill, with his new (if misunderstood) belief, his actions seemed okay at the time and, he thought, surely the most pleasant. But his idea of freedom is turned upside down. Freedom to follow the illusory self increases the mind's bondage to it. Seeing it as a sham helps the mind to ignore it and eventually allows the mind to operate freely and peacefully. This is why "situational ethics" philosophies such as, right and wrong are always relative and flexible and vary with the situation, only increase our bondage.

Appreciating the higher values isn't so easy. And it doesn't always seem to have immediate rewards. But this is the one thing that can most clearly expose the illusion of volition for what it is, along with the illusion of the self that is supposed to be exercising it. For, if volition really worked, we *could* lead a perfect life, couldn't we?

A life of indulging in the needs and wants generated by the false, conceptual self will never reveal the false self unless one finally despairs of trying to ever satisfy it and begins to question and examine why. But usually, by that time, one is too consumed by it to be able to do this.

## Meanwhile, Just Pay Attention

Watch how the thought process will rationalize what we feel compelled to do by habit and desire. In other words, it will give us a reason to do what it wants to do, whether it really makes sense or not. The pseudo-self is riddled with conflicting and contradictory needs. This is why we so often have trouble "making up our minds." Our needs frequently conflict and fight each other for fulfillment, but the strongest needs will eventually win. Futilely trying to fulfill them also feeds them and makes them stronger, like any habit. What little temporary satisfaction it gives is soon replaced with guilt and lower self-esteem.

## Grace

We have now discovered that resisting the self's needs activates them, while not resisting them makes them stronger. Doesn't this illustrate perfectly that *neither* doing nor not-doing is the only answer? Non-volition is the way out – the *only* way out. And, thank goodness it isn't something we must *do*. "You" have been removed from the situation by discovering that there isn't a "you" to do anything. Non-volitional living is simply realizing that *right now, at this moment, you are neither doing nor not-doing*. And if it seems "you" are doing, it is merely a habitual assumption. Doing just happens. It is simply the Reality, here, now. Realizing non-volitional living cuts off every option the thought process believes it had. Everything is being taken care of. It is finished. Rest. That is all that is possible.

## Free Will Or Determinism?

For ages there has been much spirited debate by scholars, philosophers and theologians over the question of whether man has free will or is subject to determinism. The joke is that it is neither. For they too have fallen for the illusion of being an object, an entity, a self. Few ever think to even question it. If there is no self then who is there to have free will? Or, for that matter, who is there to be controlled by determinism? But the debate rages like children arguing amongst themselves over whether the monster is in the closet or under the bed. Usually free will has the consensus, not because it can be proven but, well, it *feels* like we have free will. And anyhow the alternative – determinism – really amounts to fatalism and who wants that?

If the thought process is identified with a conceptual self (as it is for most of the world) then belief in free will is necessary for laws and values to have any restraint at all on people's actions (through punishment and reward). If determinism was the prevalent belief then there would be little social control, more chaos and anarchy. (Though the current trend to be a victim and blame circumstances and inanimate things seems to be leading us in that direction.)

While we live with the identification with the conceptual self, it will seem like we have free will (though it seems oddly capricious and intermittent). Then, as the illusion of the objective self and its supposed volition begins to be discovered, it may begin to look more like determinism or cause and effect. Then, when the identification with the conceptual self actually evaporates, both interdependent concepts of free will and determinism fall away because there is neither a self nor a no-self to be subject to either. What-we-are is "upstream" or prior to all such dualities. (Even space-time) True life and true actions originate from here.

Everything happens as it should. It always has.

Divine spontaneity then opens to "I just *am*."

Now, do Reality Meditation #11 once again.

# A NEW PARADIGM

*As long as I am this or that,*
*I am not all things.*
–Meister Eckhart

The so-called common-sense model of reality is that we are a separate, objective entity (a thing-in-itself) living in a pre-existing universe of separate, objective, things-in-themselves.

Most people prefer this reductionist Newtonian-type world model because it assumes an objective, quantitative, clock-work, material world that can be measured and taken apart and mathematically described and published in papers. But the findings of quantum physics contradict this model. They indicate that nothing can appear apart from the observer, that nothing exists in itself and infer that there is no such thing as an objective universe.

The new physics has been pointing to a new paradigm shift since the early 1930s. But we still haven't "got it." While the true implications of what the new physics actually means in terms of what-we-are has yet to be widely recognized, recent experiments have unequivocally proven that what we call matter isn't matter at all.

If that isn't astonishing enough, the famous "double slit" experiment has now been performed with single, whole atoms, revealing that even macro objects in the "real" world (including our own bodies), don't actually appear until they are "looked at" or "measured" by a conscious observer. Physicists call this "the collapse of the wave function," and recognize that consciousness somehow makes it happen. Until then, objects are not anything at all, and not anywhere at all, just waves of *probability*. Until recently we could safely ignore this and the alarming implications because it was just a theory and hadn't been proven. But all that has changed. We have to face the facts when things have been proven true through actual experiments, such as the famous double-slit experiment.

## *The Double-Slit Experiment*

The double-slit experiment has confirmed the undeniable role of consciousness in the manifestation of phenomenality. The experiment begins by firing streams of photons from a single source through two vertical slits in a barrier arranged side by side. On the other side of this barrier is a screen that can record (show) where each photon arrives. The result is an interference fringe pattern on the screen which appears as a series of light and dark vertical stripes, the type you would expect when two waves meet in a river. However, when *single* photons pass through the slits and reach the screen they *still* form an interference fringe pattern on the screen *as if they interfered with themselves.*

The interference fringe pattern shows that the light has traveled as if it were ripples or waves radiating out from the single source in expanding circles as when a rock is dropped into a pond. The light waves move through both slits at once, forming *two* circular wave patterns on the other side of the barrier, radiating out from each of the two slits. When these two circular waves of light reach the screen they interfere with each other just as when two expanding circles of water wave patterns meet, canceling the wave in one place where a peak and a trough meet and enlarging it in another place where two peaks or two troughs meet. This is what causes the series of light and dark vertical stripes called an interference pattern.

A simple version of this experiment was originally performed by Thomas Young early in the nineteenth century to "prove" that light was a wave, not a particle as Isaac Newton believed. Of course it is now accepted that either wave or particle behavior is manifested according to the type of experiment performed.

## *A New Version Of The Double-Slit Experiment*

In 1983 the experiment was taken further using single electrons instead of photons and it was found that if only one electron at a time is sent, the interference pattern *still forms.* As the individual electrons strike the screen they build up to form the same interference pattern as the photons did. It is as though each individual electron went through *both* slits in the barrier at the same time and interfered with itself! That is the only way the interference pattern could still appear. This means that the electron must start as a particle, but disappear and "travel" as a *wave of probabilities* and then reappear at the screen as a particle once again.

Now that seems strange enough, but the really amazing part is that if you try to check or monitor the two slits with instruments to observe which one (or both) of the slits the electron actually travels through, the light becomes an individual electron particle again at the slit where it was detected and *the interference pattern disappears!* This had also been found to be true for photons.

The act of observing actually caused the electron to manifest. Before that it didn't actually exist as a particle, there were only statistical probabilities of where it might be. The electron, by becoming a particle at the slits because it was "looked at," stops being a probability wave and must then "choose" which slit it will travel through. Thus, it no longer interferes with itself and the interference pattern no longer forms.

Physicists, in trying to establish the reality of the reductionists world of matter, have succeeded in proving the opposite. Nothing is anything in itself, but gets its meaning through relationships with everything else. And, to their puzzlement, that requires consciousness.

Quantum physics actually says that the electron wave is not really a wave of anything, but only a wave of *probabilities*. That is, the electron isn't a particle until it "arrives" (is observed) and manifests as an electron with the collapse of the wave function. Thus, the term "particle" no longer refers to something like a tiny billiard ball, as it had been pictured. Does this mean that there is no "reality?" Of course not. This is reality. It is what reality is. It is just not what we have imagined it to be.

Any act of observation of the wave, whether looked at or measured to determine its exact location in space-time, causes this collapse of the wave function.[9] This experiment proves beyond any doubt that the apparent observed and the apparent observer are linked together as one and affect the manifestation of photons, electrons and even whole atoms. MIT physicist David Pritchard successfully performed this same experiment in 1987[10] using sodium atoms rather than photons or electrons. This means that the macro world we live in (including our own bodies) works this way too.

---

9. See John Gribbin's *Schrodinger's Kittens and the search for reality*, and Michael Talbot's *Beyond the Quantum*, for good explanations of this and other recent experiments.

10. Pool, Robert, *Beams of Stuff*, Discover Magazine.

Could this possibly mean that we may actually be creating what we are looking for? Could this be the true function of faith? The peculiar reflective aspect of the collapse of the wave function may play a much larger part than is first assumed. Do we find what we are looking for because it was already there or do we find it because we are looking for it? There is much more here to explore.

## Actually Performing The EPR Thought Experiment Proves Einstein Wrong

The famous Einstein/Podolsky/Rosen "thought experiment" has actually been performed, proving non-locality and suggesting that space-time seems to be more the mechanism of phenomenal manifestation rather than some thing-in-itself.

Einstein believed in the "reality" of the material, things-in-themselves kind of world. And he thought that the newly-discovered weird probabilistic quantum effects were simply because we didn't yet know all of the reasons for that behavior.

For instance, quantum mechanics said that a particle could not have an exact position and an exact momentum at the same time because only one or the other could be measured at the collapse of the wave function. Einstein thought that in a real world of matter, a photon must actually have both qualities of position and momentum and if we couldn't measure them it was only because we didn't know how.

It was then known that if a photon pair were caused to be emitted by an atom, whatever happened to one photon would also affect the state of its "twin." If one collapsed into a particle and was found to have left polarization, the other twin must also collapse and have opposite polarization. But Einstein believed that if the two were sufficiently far enough apart, you could measure one to establish the polarization, thus collapsing the wave function. But then you could use the laws that govern collisions to determine the polarization of the twin without disturbing it, before it could be affected by the change in the first photon, since nothing could travel faster than the speed of light.

This would prove, Einstein believed, that the light waves really did possess "material reality" in the form of both momentum and position. At that time however it was impossible to actually perform such an experiment, so it was referred to as a "thought experiment" used to illustrate Einstein's view.

In 1982, physicist Alain Aspect of the University of Paris successfully performed that experiment by making two simultaneous measurements on pairs of photons that were emitted in a single event from the same atom and sent in opposite directions. And they did retain their reciprocal relationship, proving Einstein wrong.

This experiment has been verified by others beyond any doubt. Somehow the second particle was affected instantaneously by the changes to the first particle no matter what the distance. Either the communication between them was faster than the speed of light, or distance does not really exist and is an illusion.

This is referred to as "non-locality" by physicists, meaning not in a place, inferring that place or distance is an illusion, that everything is "here" or that *all* is local. Maybe it should be called "non-distance" instead. And, of course, the "separate reality" of the photon in terms of possessing its own momentum and position (while it is a probability wave) in space-time is disproved.

## Our World Model Will Change To A Non-Dual Paradigm

These new physics experiments are forcing us to drastically change our Newtonian, mechanistic world model of separate, independent objects existing as things in themselves, operating together like a huge clock-work.

How does a photon or electron or an atom *know* when it is being observed and then manifest? The observer-observed "real world" Newtonian belief system cannot answer this. But if the observer and the observed are a conceptual construct from an observ-*ing* in consciousness, the answer is more simple. There are no waves or particles, just raw percepts appearing in consciousness and ultimately interpreted as "things out there" and "me here."

I would then like to suggest to physicists everywhere (and nowhere) that the observer and the observed are not two separate self-existing things, but that *both* seer and seen are spontaneously appearing in consciousness as percepts but are being interpreted as two separate things because of the conceptual thought process using the dualistic world model.

I would also like to suggest that there are *not* a lot of separate little consciousnesses in a lot of separate bodies: the observed and the observer are not two but the same. They are both mental constructs created from subjective percepts. The secret that the physicists have not yet realized is that they appear in consciousness as simply an "observ-*ing*" which is then interpreted by split-mind (the dualistic thought process) as observer and observed.

We are not actually seeing a pre-existing world when we "observe" it, we are actually spontaneously *creating* it using the conceptual extensions of space-time, manifesting it and our own bodies, from moment to moment.

For me, these experiments prove our *eternal life* – not as separate individual entities, but as the "One Pure Consciousness" whose ultimate source is the Absolute. This is the source of our sense of "I am," the *knowing* that I am, here, now. Everything else appears in this awareness, even the perceptions of a "me."

These experiments are pointing us to the breathtaking, liberating revelation that all of "this" is actually the same "stuff." That all there is, is consciousness. And that's what we really are! It must also be all the *same* consciousness – not many individual consciousnesses created in many individual bodies as we have been taught (because our own bodies are being created in consciousness, not the other way around). It is only the phenomenal appearances that are different, making it seem that there are many separate consciousnesses.

We are all the same sense of "I am" in which many viewpoints are appearing. As a crude analogy, imagine one large TV screen on which many picture-in-picture programs are being shown simultaneously. We take ourselves for one of the programs when we are the whole screen. We don't even notice the screen because it is the clear background upon which everything is appearing and we are caught up in what is appearing on it. In other words, we don't notice we are consciousness because it is the clear background within which everything is appearing and we (actually the autonomic thought process) are caught up in what is appearing. And this same thought process believes we are some-thing (the body) that is appearing in it.

The mind has identified with this body as what we are. If that wasn't bad enough, it has also imagined another separate, individual *thing* called a "me," mysteriously inhabiting and operating this body like the driver of a car. And this "me" is not alone. There is also supposed to be a separate, individual *thing* called a "spirit," a separate individual *thing* called a "soul," an individual *thing* called a mind, an individual *thing* called an ego, etc., all crowded in there, all jostling for the title "me." Sometimes one of these are what we are, other times they are something we have or use – whatever is imagined at the time. Isn't this just a bit confusing when you stop to examine it?

When watching a movie notice that the camera always has a location in space and time from which the scene is viewed – otherwise nothing could appear. Likewise, an apparent sensory viewpoint in space-time is necessary for phenomenality to appear and to "interact" with it. How else could it be? That is the purpose of the body. But that does not mean that the sensory viewpoint is where consciousness is or where we are or where any "me" is. Just as when you are dreaming, consciousness is not *in* your dreamed body, that's just the viewpoint, the perceptual location where the world is manifested using the five senses via space-time. Rather, the *whole dream* is consciousness. Everything which is appearing in consciousness, *is* consciousness.

Consciousness is not in space-time, rather space-time is in consciousness. Space-time is not something in itself. It is a basic *conceptual process* or mechanism which consciousness uses to project "the world" using the three spatial extensions and one temporal extension as duration.

Our seemingly separate, objective world as well as our separate, objective individuality is simply an illusion of the conceptual thought process because of our learned Newtonian world model.

This, of course, doesn't mean that the world does not exist, or that we do not exist. It simply means that what is called the world (and us) are not as the mind has interpreted them.

We will soon be forced to move from the dualistic Newtonian world model to the true non-dual reality. Beyond the obvious liberating effects, this new paradigm opens vast new possibilities for exploring time and space because, when we understand what-we-are, we will no longer be imprisoned by materiality or space or time.

The new physics is telling us, quite clearly, that we are not *in* the universe, but rather that the universe *is in us*.

# THE REAL
# POSSIBILITIES

*"All the teachings of all the masters of all the schools of liberation, not only Buddhic, Vedantic, and Taoist, but Semitic also – as, witness, 'Not my will but Thine, O Lord' – consists in attempts by means of knowledge, practices, and manoeuvres to free the pseudo-individual from the chains of volition, for when that is abandoned no bondage remains.*

*"The purest doctrines, such as those of Ramana Maharshi, Padma Sambhava, Huang Po and Shen Hui, just teach us that it is sufficient by analysis utterly to comprehend that there is no entity which could have effective volition, that an apparent act of volition when in accord with the inevitable can only be a vain gesture and, when in discord, the fluttering of a caged bird against the bars of his cage. When he knows that, then at last he has peace and is glad."*

– Wei Wu Wei.
*All Else Is Bondage*

The ideal form of existence would be one in which both the linear (horizontal) and non-linear (vertical) aspects of cognition could be readily accessible to conscious awareness. This has been called "reintegration," and is associated with the dissolution of the identification with the pseudo-self. It was possibly the increasing reliance upon the conceptual thought processes (split-mind) that brought about the submersion and loss of awareness of this unconscious, non-linear, non-dual aspect of the mental processes. This could well be what has been, along with the identification with the pseudo-self, labeled as the Biblical "fall of man." It certainly seems reasonable to equate this "fall" into a lower dimension from the actual to the conceptual, with a major shift in identity and understanding. This is even more plausible when it is realized that the terms "the knowledge of good and evil" (Genesis 3:1) have meaning *only* in relation to a self, that is, how events affect the perceived needs and desires of an individual, objective entity.

My experience related earlier was not the ultimate "liberation" of awakening but just a facet of an ever-deepening and wondrous unfolding of this understanding. And for some time it had a puzzling effect. Instead of greater understanding, I had no conceptual understanding for a while, especially of non-volitional living. It dissolved all of what I thought of as "my understanding." It was a version of the "dark night of the soul," and was extremely disorienting and disturbing. Then, very gradually, the original understanding began to open again, but with a vast new dimension.

For many, after first recognizing what-we-are, there is a ripening of understanding, a recursive revelation – until one is free to pass back and forth between realms and dimensions: time/timelessness

– space/spacelessness – things/no-thing – local/non-local. This is actually approached via the negation of both opposites of such dualisms. The negation is "neither/nor," (neither this nor that) – the non-dual.

You don't need to have an experience similar to mine. Such "spiritual experiences" are not necessary for insight and should not be actively sought. Though, in the beginning, it may be hard not to look for something similar to affirm your insight. But rest assured, your own experience of insight, when it happens, will not need any confirmation; it will be so obvious, so right, it will be outstanding in itself as an important turning point in your life.

Just in case the most important points have not been stated clearly enough, and at the risk of redundancy, and also for the sake of dear Wei Wu Wei who might well say; "It's once more into the breach." – let me reiterate:

All there is, is consciousness. There are no individual people, no actual things. Nor are there a lot of "little consciousnesses," such as one for you and one for me. There is only One. And yet this is not really even a one, as there is no "thing" that is consciousness. The "you's" and the "me's" are also this consciousness. *Nor is there anyone to know this or to act on this nor to use this to control themselves or anyone else through this.* Yet, we can say, I am. This is reality.

At this very moment, Consciousness is "living" us all and is what-we-are. But neither is there any "me" to be "given up" or even any "me" to rest in this. We are already all of this phenomenally and none of this noumenally.

It is only because of the conceptualizing of arising percepts that there seem to be separate things-in-themselves. The same thing happens with sleeping dreams, but, when we awaken, we realize that it was just perceptions arising in consciousness. Nothing more. This, the living dream, is no different.

What we have believed to be the world is simply a "consensus reality." Because of mindset some may tend to interpret the things in this book in ways I never intended or imagined, no matter how hard I have tried to prevent it. Not purposely, but because the conditioned mind will automatically try to make it into something familiar.

In any event, if we could stop jumping to the conclusion that we are an objective volitional entity and begin to discover our true origin, we could then start making real progress as sentient beings. The mind's astounding abilities could be used in much more intelligent and productive ways (as they may have been in the distant past).

It is now up to you, dear readers, to further explore the infinite miracle of what-we-are. To open new doors to new un-utilized abilities and insights now available to those who dare and to those who must and those who are urged on by a never-ending sense of wonder.

Whether or not you get anything else from this book, I hope you take away at least this fundamental truth: find the tacit sense of being, the bare, silent sense of "am," the awareness with which you are knowing this moment – pure consciousness – the sense of presence. Focus on this alone and learn to appreciate it. This is the miracle of miracles. We live with it every moment but it is invisible, unnoticed and unknown to us because we do not realize that it *is* the moment, every moment. This is the source and substance of all that appears. That appreciation will grow into love, and that love will become bliss which will pervade the entire universe.

# BIBLIOGRAPHY

## Web Sites

There is now a web site devoted entirely to Wei Wu Wei and his works –
*THE 'WEI WU WEI' ARCHIVES:*
http://www.weiwuwei.8k.com

This author's own website offering his book, *What Am I: A Study In Non-Volitional Living,* and offering all of Wei Wu Wei's books currently available:
http://www.galensharp.com

## Books Written By Terence James Stannus Gray

NOTE: All the books by Wei Wu Wei, listed below with the original publisher have now been republished by Sentient Publications and are currently available.

Editions originally published under the pen name of O.O.O. Now published by Sentient Publications under the pen name of Wei Wu Wei.

*Unworldly Wise: As The Owl Remarked To The Rabbit.*
Hong Kong University Press, Hong Kong, 1974.

## Under the pen name of Wei Wu Wei

*All Else Is Bondage: Non-Volitional Living.* Hong Kong University Press, Hong Kong, 1964.

*Ask The Awakened,* The Negative Way. Little Brown And Company, 1963.

*Fingers Pointing Towards The Moon: Reflections Of A Pilgrim On The Way.* Hong Kong University Press, Hong Kong, 1958.

*Open Secret.* Hong Kong University Press, Hong Kong, 1965.

*Posthumous Pieces.* Hong Kong University Press, Hong Kong, 1968.

*The Tenth Man, The Great Joke (Which Made Lazarus Laugh).* Hong Kong University Press, Hong Kong, 1966.

*Why Lazarus Laughed: The Essential Doctrine, Zen - Advaita - Tantra.* Hong Kong University Press, Hong Kong, 1960.

## Translations By Terence Gray

Translated from the French to English by Terence Grey, aka. Wei Wu Wei:

Benoit, Hurbert. *The Supreme Doctrine, Psychological Studies in Zen Thought*. Viking Press, New York, 1955.

### Humanity's Next Step?

Eddington, Sir Arthur. *The Nature Of The Physical World*. University Of Michigan Press, Ann Arbor, 1974.

Heisenburg, Werner. *Physics And Beyond*. Harper & Row, New York, 1971.

Blofeld, John, Translator. *The Zen Teachings of Huang Po*. p. 127, p. 108, Grove Press, New York, 1958.

### What Is A World Model?

Bolles, Edmund Blair. *A Second Way Of Knowing*. Prentiss Hall Press, 1991.

Ryan, John K., Translator. *The Confessions Of St. Augustine*. Image Books, Doubleday & Company, Garden City, 1960. See p. 287 Ch 14, What Is Time?

Doresse, Jean. *The Secret Books Of The Egyptian Gnostics*. (*The Gospel According To Thomas*,) MJF Books, New York, 1986.

GALEN SHARP

## The Origin Of All Things

Harding, Douglas C. *The Science Of The First Person.*
Shollond Publications, Nacton, Ipswich, 1974.

## A New Paradigm

Eddington, Sir Arthur. *The Nature Of The Physical
World.* University Of Michigan Press, Ann Arbor, 1974.

Gribben, John. *Schrödinger's Kittens: And The Search
For Reality.* Little Brown, Boston, 1995.

Talbot, Michael. *Beyond The Quantum.* Bantam Books,
New York, 1998.

Pool, Robert. *Beams Of Stuff.* Discover Magazine, pp.
104-107, December, 1997.

Heisenburg, Werner. *Physics And Beyond.* Harper &
Row, New York, 1971.

## Additional Sources:

Balsekar, Ramesh S. *Pointers From Nisargadatta
Maharaj.* Acorn Press, Durham, 1982.

Benoit, Hubert. *The Supreme Doctrine.* Viking Press,
New York, 1959.

Blackney, Raymond, Translator. *Meister Eckhart.* Harper & Row, New York, 1941.

Blackney, Raymond, Translator. *Meister Eckhart: The Celebrated 14th Century Mystic And Scholastic,* Harper & Row, New York, 1941.

Blofeld, John, Translator. *The Zen Teachings of Huang Po.* Grove Press, New York, 1958.

Bloefeld, John, Translator. *The Zen Teachings of Hui Hai On Sudden Illumination.* Samuel Weiser, New York, 1962.

Bucke, R. M. *Cosmic Consciousness.* E.P. Dutton, New York, 1969.

Chung Yan, Chang, Translator. *Original Teachings Of Ch'an Buddhism.* Vintage Books, New York, 1969.

Dunn, Jean, Editor. *Consciousness And The Absolute: TheFinal Talks Of Sri Nisargadatta Maharaj.* Acorn Press, Durham, 1994.

Dunn, Jean, Editor. *Prior To Consciousness.* Acorn Press, Durham, 1983.

Dunn, Jean, Editor. *Seeds Of Consciousness.* Acorn Press, Durham, 1982.

Harding, Douglas C. *On Having No Head, A Contribution To Zen In The West.* Arkana, London, 1986.

Harding, Douglas C. *The Hierarchy Of Heaven And Earth.* Faber & Faber, Ltd., London, 1952.

Osborne, Arthur. *The Teachings Of Ramana Maharshi.* Samuel Weiser, New York, 1962.

Price, A.F., and Wong Mou-Lam, translators. *The Diamond Sutra & The Sutra of Hui Neng.* Shambala, Boulder, 1969.

Reps, Paul, Compiler. *Zen Flesh, Zen Bones.* Anchor Books, Garden City, 1964.

Schloegl, Irmgard, Translator. *The Zen Teachings of Rinzai,* Shambala, Berkley, 1976.

Scofield, C.I. Editor. *The Scofield Reference Bible.* Oxford University Press, New York, 1969.

Sri Nisargadatta Maharaj. *I Am That.* Acorn Press, Durham, 1988.

Suzuki, D.T. *Manual Of Zen Buddhism.* Ballantine Books, New York, 1974.

Suzuki, D.T. *The Zen Doctrine Of No Mind.* Samuel
Weiser, New York, 1969.

*The Laymen's Parallel New Testament.* Zonderman,
Grand Rapids, 1970.

Walters, Clifton, Translator. *The Cloud of Unknowing.*
Penguin, Baltimore, 1944.

# ABOUT THE AUTHOR

Galen Sharp is a sculptor and author. In the 1970s he began a correspondence with the brilliant and enigmatic non-duality sage Terrence Stannus Gray, who wrote under the name Wei Wu Wei, that was to last several years. His teaching was to completely transform Galen's worldview and life. This book is the fruit of Wei Wu Wei's influence on a young seeker after truth.

Made in the USA
Lexington, KY
02 May 2013